Give Love A Chance

Book 2

By Maxine Ferris

Cover Art By Betsy Morphew

*To Barb,
Have a good read!
Maxine Ferris
2018*

Kids At Heart Publishing LLC
PO Box 492
Milton, IN 47357
765-478-5873
www.kidsatheartpublishing.com

© 2018 Maxine Ferris. All rights reserved.

No part of this book may be reproduced, stored in a retrieval system, or transmitted by any means without the written permission of the author.

First published by Kids At Heart Publishing LLC 7/10/2018
ISBN # 978-1-946171-23-8
Library of Congress Control Number: 2018952823

Printed in the United States of America
Milton, Indiana

This book printed on acid-free paper.

To order more copies of this book go to
www.kidsatheartpublishing.com

The books at Kids At Heart Publishing feature turn the page technology. No batteries or charging required.

DEDICATION:

This book is dedicated to the men and women who, after the age of eighty, continue to embrace new challenges, debate contemporary issues and learn new things. It celebrates the elders who dare to navigate the stormy waters of a new career and to feel the heady joy and pride of achieving a personal goal. Hopefully, this book will inspire others to challenge and renew themselves throughout their octogenarian years…and beyond.

"Responsibility for the content of this work lies entirely with the author. The content of this work does not represent the official views or policies of Michigan State University. Neither Michigan State University nor any person acting on its behalf may be held responsible for any use which may be made of the information contained herein. Any resemblance to real persons, living or dead is purely coincidental."

"Responsibility for the content of this work lies entirely with the author. The content of this work does not represent the official views or policies of Purdue University. Neither Purdue University nor any person acting on its behalf may be held responsible for any use which may be made of the information contained herein. Any resemblance to real persons, living or dead is purely coincidental.

ACKNOWLEDGEMENTS

Writing a sequel to "Let Love Happen" was not on my bucket list; but thanks to reader encouragement, it is now in print. The support of family members, readers and friends made "Give Love a Chance" a reality! A special thanks is due my husband, Jake Ferris, for proofreading and other technical help.

The assistance of Publisher Shelley Davis and Cover Artist, Betsy Morphew, made the process go smoothly. Access to on-line resources in the public domain were a help in verifying current information pertaining to Mozambique and the status of research on Jatropha. The assistance of staff and the opportunity to observe classes at the Montessori Radmoor School is much appreciated. But once again, special tribute must be paid to my friend, Katha J. Heinze, who not only served as a most professional editor, but whose wise counsel as "critic in residence" ensured that the narrative and characters were realistic, and the book was not didactic.

Maxine Ferris

CHAPTER ONE

Yes, the words, "giddy excitement" and "heady anticipation" fittingly describe the atmosphere at the house on Ottawa Drive! And why not? The honeymooners were expected to arrive momentarily. Five-year-old twins, Michael and Mia, were ecstatic and could hardly contain their exuberance in having their daddy and their new mommy back home.

The twins' grandmothers had laughingly called them their "fetch and carry helpers" since they had been most helpful in moving chairs, arranging the tables and bringing needed items from the kitchen to the patio and backyard for the "Welcome Home" picnic. The Gerber grandparents, Peg's folks, had arrived shortly after lunch and brought part of the "fixings" from the farm. Papa Gerber joined Ian's dad in checking out the grill to make sure it was in working order, and now it was time for the two men to leave for the airport to provide taxi service for the returning travelers.

"Everything looks festive," remarked Kate Mahoney, Ian's mother.

"That it does," responded Peg's mother, Rosemary.

"I'm glad we decided to serve a different menu!" Kate said.

"I agree," Rosemary added. "The gazpacho and melon

cucumber salad will be a nice change from the standard baked beans and potato salad."

"Grilling k-bobs instead of brats and burgers will be a hit too."

"I hear Libby is bringing her yummy onion dill bread," offered Rosemary.

"Yes, and Jodie is picking up some of that new peach ice cream at the campus dairy store to go with her cupcakes. Everyone should be well fed."

"Hey," Rosemary said, glancing toward the house next door, "I think I hear the pastor driving in, so everyone should be here shortly."

The twins came racing outdoors shouting, "Mimi, G-ma it's time! The clock in the kitchen says so! Papa and Papa G should be back any minute."

"Right you are," confirmed the grandmothers. "Let's go around front and admire that great 'Welcome Home' sign the two of you made."

The four had barely turned the corner when the Gerber SUV pulled up to unload its cargo. What a welcome sight! The five-year-olds were caught up in an encompassing family hug that left many with tears spilling down their cheeks. Everyone began talking at once. What a joyful sound!

The luggage was brought inside by the two grandfathers, and the grandmothers urged a bit of relaxation before the invited guests arrived.

"Aren't you exhausted?" asked Rosemary.

"No, not really," Peg laughed. "How could we be tired with THIS reception?"

"Jet lag always seems to be worse when you're heading East," added Ian. "I guess we were too excited to notice, in any case."

"I'll bet you're hungry, Miss Peggy," chimed in Mia.

"Oops, I mean…Mommy!" The child blushed as she acknowledged her mistake and got a big hug from Peg.

"We've been practicing saying 'Mommy,' interjected her twin. Wait til you see the special picnic we're having in the backyard as soon as Libby, her family and the Allens get here."

After Peg and Ian had a little time to freshen-up, they joined their parents, the children, and their next-door neighbors, the Lanes…all of whom had assembled in the backyard.

Just then, another round of "'Welcome Home!' greeted Peg and Ian as their close friends, Jodie and Ben Allen rounded the house with their son, BJ.

After hugging the newcomers, Ian glanced at the picnic table…laden with food. "I'm really hungry," he said. "We were both too excited to eat much today."

"That's for sure…but where's Ida?" Peg asked looking around for the children's babysitter and dear friend. Why isn't she here?"

Ian's mother responded, "She returns from Denver tomorrow. She hated to miss your homecoming, but her grandson's birthday party was this afternoon. You know how much she loves seeing those grandchildren and hates to miss her family celebrations."

As everyone began loading their plates, the questions rained down from all quarters. "How was Italy?" "Did you enjoy the side trips to Innsbruck and Salzburg?" "Did you locate any of our ancestors?" "How was the surprise finale that Ian arranged?"

The newlyweds looked at each other and laughed, "Where do we begin?" they asked in unison. "We saw and did so many different things."

"No, Mom, we didn't do any genealogy work," began Peggy. "We left that for you and Dad to do on your trip to Germany and Austria."

Mia interrupted, "We saw and did a lot of different things too, didn't we, Mikey?"

"Yes," responded her twin, "Mimi took us to the campus to feed the ducks; and Papa gave us a ride on a golf cart. That was lots of fun."

"Don't forget all the stuff we did on the farm," piped up his sister. "Papa G helped me lead Lady Long Legs around the barnyard, three times; and G-ma and I canned dilly beans."

"After I picked the beans," reminded her brother.

Ian laughed, "Mommy and I knew you'd have a great time with your grandparents while we were gone. We were sure that you'd have lots of stories to tell when we got back… and we can't wait to hear all of them!"

Turning to the others, Ian said, "I have to say, our stay in Bergamo was outstanding! The Montessori Center is certainly impressive. Now I know why Peg is such a superbly trained Directress!"

"Thanks, honey," Peg smiled at her husband. "The Center continues to be ahead of the educational game, even while they remain faithful to the guiding principles of Dr. Maria Montessori. They have integrated many new technologies into their instruction and are always adapting the curriculum as current and future needs unfold."

"Did any of your classmates return for the special program?" her mom asked.

"A few, but not many. Some did send letters that were shared at one of the sessions."

"The Center was fascinating, but so was the city, itself," Ian continued. "I really loved the old part of the city. It's retained its charm while the rest of Bergamo is very modern, like any European city its size."

"Did you rent a car during your trip?" asked Ben Allen.

"No, actually we did a lot of walking, used public transportation and took the train when we went into Austria," explained Ian. "It worked out fine, since we didn't have a lot of luggage to carry around."

"How were the accommodations?" Jodie asked.

"Homey and pleasant, as small European guest houses tend to be," responded her former roommate. "You would have loved them too!"

"Did the conference at the training center have a theme?" wondered Rod Lane, a history teacher.

"Leave it to you to ask," laughed the new Mrs. Mahoney. "I thought it was perfect: Embracing the Past, Enriching the Present, Envisioning the Future."

"We also appreciated our tour of the Bergamo Cathedral, Pastor Becky," added Peg turning to her neighbor. "Walking through all four of the ancient gates that access the old city was a humbling experience. It certainly gave us a sense of the city's early history and its concerns for safety from invaders."

"I'm sure you ate well and had some wonderful things to see and do in your other two lovely destinations in the Alps," remarked Ian's dad, Big Mike.

"Did you see any kids wearing those leather pants?" inquired young Mike.

"A few did," responded his dad, "but not many."

Peggy continued her husband's thought, "A lot of men in the Tyrolean Folk Show we attended in Innsbruck wore lederhosen. In fact, all the performers wore traditional costumes. It was really cool…and we loved the knee-clapping music. Since we walked around a lot there and took a two-hour walking tour in Salzburg, I was glad I had a pair of good walking shoes."

"Did they sing any songs that you knew?" Mia wanted to know.

"Yes, not only there but at a free Mozart concert in Mirabel Gardens, too," Peggy responded. "The closing number was very familiar, since that's where Maria and the children sang 'Do-Re-Me' in . . ."

"I know!" the twins called out in unison then glanced at each other, "We know lots of songs from 'The Sound of Music!'"

The adults smiled, and the Lane's teenage daughter, Libby explained, "While you were gone, we saw a re-run of that movie and wondered if you felt like you were in Von Trapp family territory."

"That we did," was the reply.

"We forgot to tell you that Libby took us to the place where she and Uncle Jake work," Michael said excitedly. "It's an animal hospital, and they take care of sick animals. Uncle Jake is going to be an animal doctor."

"I might want to be that kind of doctor too," reflected his twin.

Rosemary interjected, "Peg, you and Ian will be delighted to read the wonderful journals the children faithfully kept every day. They recorded each day's activities in both words and drawings."

"That they did," added their other grandmother. The twins beamed, pleased that their efforts were being recognized.

"We'll want to see them first thing tomorrow…and hear stories about what you did each day," said Peg and Ian as they nodded their approval.

"I'm curious how the surprise trip to Vienna went," wondered Kate.

"I was absolutely thrilled!" responded her daughter-in-law. "Now I know why it's the favorite city of so many people! Meeting your former exchange student, Karl, and his wife, Gretchen, was the perfect finale for our unforgettable two weeks!"

"Mother, they insisted that we stay with them in their attractive little house near the Danube. One afternoon we took a river cruise. Our Montessori Directress was quite the hit with a class of schoolchildren who were eager to engage her in conversation. It was a great way for them to practice their English."

Peggy went on, "While in Vienna we took the 'Hop-on-Hop-off' bus tour of the city and were amazed at how well the old and new are blending side-by-side. But probably the entertainment highlight was the summer concert in the garden of the beautiful Schoenbrunn Palace. We didn't get to tour it but heard a wonderful program of Strauss waltzes performed by the city's world-famous orchestra."

"What a treat that must have been," reflected Mrs. Gerber. "Remember how we used to watch their New Year's performance on tv, Peggy?"

Just then, Michael jumped up and asked, "Can we go in and show BJ the big Lego castle we built this morning before he goes home?"

"Of course, Mikey, our picnic is about finished," came the reply. So off ran the twins with BJ close behind.

Peg picked up the former conversation thread. "Hey, Mom, that reminds me…remember the hard time your three sons always gave you and Dad when you insisted on demonstrating your dancing skills as though you were competing in a waltz contest? We always had a good laugh at your expense!"

"Boys will be boys," commented her dad shaking his head.

"Several years ago, we were in Vienna, too. We actually

spent one Christmas holiday there visiting Karl and his parents after he had stayed with us for a year in Washington," Kate recalled, then turned to her husband. "Remember that long red-carpeted staircase leading to the concert hall in the palace, Mike?"

"I'd like to do a repeat of that experience," said her husband, the singer in the family.

"We tried to imagine the meaningful experiences you were having, but we're so glad that the reality was even better than we hoped! We'll look forward to hearing the "rest of the story" another time," Kate said, standing and beginning to gather serving bowls.

"And I, for one, am looking forward to seeing the pictures you obviously took," added the pastor.

Just then, the youngsters returned to the gathering darkness of the yard…and noting their drooping eyelids, the adults hastened to clear the tables and return the chairs to the patio. Good-byes, thanks and hugs were exchanged.

After a quick clean up, the Gerbers left with the Allens, their hosts for the night. The senior Mahoneys went next door to spend the night as guests of the Lanes, leaving the newly-formed family alone for the first time. In the morning, the two older couples planned to take off for a short holiday in the Traverse City area, thankful for the bond that now existed as an extended family.

Peg and Ian helped the exhausted twins get ready for bed. After the kids brushed their teeth, and the family read a book together; the four of them joined hands and knelt in prayer to thank God for their safe return and the miracle that had brought them together as a family.

CHAPTER TWO

After a day of unpacking, sharing the precious daily journals faithfully kept by Mike and Mia, and surprising the children with several small gifts; Ian and Peggy were eager to return to their respective workplaces and see what had transpired in their absences.

"I can't believe that we actually forgot about our jobs," observed Peg.

"That's a fact," agreed her husband. "Now it's time to get back to reality. Are you sure you want to take both of these ruffians with you?" he said motioning to the twins.

"Of course," was their mommy's reply. "They're going to have a great time working in the school's little market selling produce and items made during summer school activities in the green house."

"Have a good day at the office, Daddy," shouted the twins as they climbed into the red Volt, securing their seatbelts. Then, off they headed to Ojibwa Montessori School.

As Ian stepped into his office on the campus of Michigan State University, he smiled as he recalled his first visit to this office just one year ago. Having such a large well-appointed office had been quite unexpected. He fondly recalled how the twins had helped him carry in his books and office supplies. It really had pleased him that they chose to spend the afternoon playing professor. He'd never forget how amused he was that Mike had questioned him about actually eating flowers. He'd have to remember to find some to take home for dessert one of these days.

What a change a year had made, and not just in his marital status. His "in box" was almost empty, a sign that they were now an almost completely paper-free office. Electronic correspondence had really taken over although he found that the content of the messages remained about the same. He checked the calendar on his Iphone and nodded his head in recognition: an upcoming faculty meeting, a seminar with grad students and a family picnic at the park.

He was pleased to find confirmation that the funding team from Washington had agreed to his proposed dates for their session in Michigan and indicated pleasure that he had selected the English Inn in Eaton Rapids as the venue for the meeting as well as for their over-night stay. Also, it seemed that his three graduate assistants were eager to get busy with the next phase of their work on the Jatropha plant research project. They had scheduled several hours with him at the start of next week.

He was interrupted by a knock on the door. Kevin and Jay, two of his colleagues, had stopped by to welcome him home and set up a meeting to share their plans for the educational outreach they would be conducting in Mozambique, thanks to a modest grant from the USAID after Ian's inclusion of their representatives on his data collection trip in January.

He thought how amazing it was that the three of them had become so congenial after a rocky start last fall. The two "locals" had resented the newcomer's status and perceived unearned perks. However, with Ian's help, their major research proposal – which had been stalled for some time – appeared to have secured funding, at last. Last fall, embarrassed by their initial behavior toward Ian, they had apologized and took steps to become participating partners on the Mozambique project.

They had barely left the office when an attractive young woman appeared in the open doorway. "Hello, Professor, may I interrupt you for a few minutes?" she asked.

"Of course. Come right in and have a seat," Ian welcomed her, struggling for a name, although the woman looked familiar. "I've just been reviewing my calendar."

"You don't recognize me, do you?" she asked.

"I, I , , ," stammered her host. "It's been some time, hasn't it?"

She laughed. "That's true! You were in Africa when I came for my interview last winter. By the way, I never really thanked you for recommending me for the position here at State. Congratulations on your recent marriage. You certainly look happy!"

Ian smiled and shook his head. "Of course! Welcome to Michigan, Dr. Jordan Taylor. Just look at you…all grown up with a new PhD in your pocket and a faculty appointment in the Department of Horticulture! Congratulations! The faculty at Texas A & M must be delighted to have you placed so well so quickly. My Dad will look forward to meeting you."

"That goes for me too. I'd forgotten that Dr. Mahoney was in horticulture too, or maybe I never made the connection between the two of you. His reputation as a department chair was legendary."

"If you have time, I'd like to hear about your appointment and the nature of your work at MSU. Are you still trying to perfect that ornamental grass that had your attention earlier?"

"Certainly," she responded as she relaxed in her chair. "I have a two-way split appointment – 80% research and 20% teaching; and yes, I'm still pursuing an answer to the grass problem."

"Your split appointment is similar to mine, which works well for me, but Dad would argue that a three or four-way split is even better. He sincerely believes that outreach and international dimensions are important components in a professor's growth and development."

"Interesting assessment," Jordan responded thoughtfully, "I imagine the two of you have some thought-provoking discussions. Do your parents still live in this area?"

"No, they retired near Hilton Head, so he can golf nearly year-round, but they visit often…need to see the grandkids, you know. How about your folks?" Ian asked, "do they still live in Indiana?"

"There's only Mom, now. Dad was killed by a hit-and-run driver when I was a sophomore at Purdue, and my mother is no longer in Indiana."

"I'm sorry that I never knew that about your dad. It must have been tough to lose a parent at that age," Ian said sympathetically, thinking how ironic it was that she had lost a parent almost the same way he had lost his first wife.

"It was a very significant loss, since we were always very close. I never really shared much about my personal life, especially with my professors. I was pretty self-absorbed in those days. As I think back, I must have been a real pain in the you-know-what. I was obsessed with doing well, being the best student in my classes. I paid little attention to how I looked and did my best to avoid socializing with anybody."

"What I remember is that you were always on time for class, stayed late, frantically took notes, wrote great papers and aced the exams."

"That's all true," Jordan laughed. "As a first-year graduate student, I wanted to make sure that I was successful. Besides, I'd heard that you had really tough expectations, and I guess I wanted to impress you."

"Like you, I was trying to live up to expectations, myself," Ian admitted. "The year when you were in my class, my personal life was in shambles, so I didn't try to make personal connections, either. I just tried to stay focused on making sure that you students got your money's worth, which in my mind meant pushing everyone to his or her academic limits. With you that was easy! I remember that you were eager to learn everything you possibly could. Your resume is testimony to the fact that you achieved that goal."

"Coming from you that means a lot…from others, not so much. While I was a student, I tried to sort of make myself invisible; but unfortunately, that only drew negative attention to me. I'm sure lots of people on campus thought I was really odd."

"It was hard to overlook your excellence in the classroom, Jordan," Ian said supportively. "Now on another note, have you found a place to live? My wife, Peggy, is sure to ask. By the way, I'll have her give you a call about coming to dinner soon."

"I'd like that, but no fussing please!" Joran insisted. "In answer to your question, 'yes,' I'm sub-letting a small house in what I think they call the 'flower pot district' of East Lansing. The owners are on a sabbatical in England and wanted someone who would care for their house, their plants and their garden. There is a small attached apartment where the professor's mother lives. She's a very active 80-year-old, but they don't really want her to be totally alone."

"That sounds like a great option until you get to know the area," Ian offered. "I was able to buy the house my family owned when I was a child…so for me the move really seemed as if I was coming home. It's on the Red Cedar Golf Course, but, unfortunately, I don't play. Do you?"

"Not really," she admitted. "Hey, before I leave, I wanted to ask if you'd take a look at my Experiment Station research proposal to see if it's sufficiently detailed? I've never completed this particular form before and want to get it right the first time."

"Why, of course!" he agreed. "Just send it to me as soon as it's ready for review. Is it a continuation of your doctoral work or have you decided to pursue other research?"

"My dissertation allowed me to discard one plan that didn't work out. Now I want to pursue another idea that I've had," Jordan explained. "I'd like to give ornamental grasses at least one more shot before I shift gears. I'm interested in what you're discovering in your Jatropha plant work. After all, your weed and my grass may not be too far removed from one another genetically."

"Who knows? Could be!" Ian agreed.

Jordan stood up, "Thanks for seeing me without an appointment on your first day back. I'm sure there's a lot of catching up you plan to do today. I'll look forward to meeting your wife and getting reacquainted with those cute twins. I couldn't help noticing the pictures on your desk...they certainly have grown up!"

"How could I have forgotten?" Ian said, embarrassed. "Once when I was in a real bind, you volunteered to babysit for them when they were toddlers."

"I was glad to help in an emergency 'though I must confess, I was terrified!" she laughed. "What if something had happened to them on MY watch…and YOU, my professor! Here's my new business card, if you need to get in touch with me. I'll send you the proposal after the week-end."

"So glad to reconnect!" Ian said offering a warm handshake. "I know that hiring you was a real smart move by my colleagues down the hall! Stay in touch; the door is always open."

After she left, he thought, "Oh my goodness, I would never have recognized that professional young woman as being Jordan Taylor, the brilliant, rather plain-looking grad student I had in class back at A & M. What a difference a few years and a little confidence make! I can't wait to tell Peg about her. If anyone can do it, Peg will be sure to figure out the story of her transformation. There must surely be an interesting story in there somewhere."

CHAPTER THREE

The twins chattered away as they headed for their school, eager to get started on their shift at the roadside market. Spending a lot of the summer learning new things in the school's greenhouse had been great fun. They had not only learned about growing and caring for plants but also how to use them to make new items that could be sold at the school market.

Peg waved as the children trotted off to receive their instructions, then headed to her classroom. "Good," she said aloud as she noticed the fresh coat of paint on the walls and glanced at the furnishings amassed in the middle of the room. She paused for a moment and thought about some of the classroom configurations she had heard about in Bergamo.

Before she could begin the project, though, two people came through the doorway. "Hi, Grace. It's good to see you and great to be back. I'm excited to begin preparing for the new year." Peggy hurried over to Grace Foster, the Ojibwa School Administrator.

"Welcome back, Peggy! We really missed having you on staff this summer," Grace said, giving Peg a quick hug. "And congratulations on your beautiful wedding! I hope the European honeymoon was perfect. When Dave and I got married 25 years ago, we went camping in the Upper Peninsula and did battle with the black flies."

Grace paused, then indicated the young man standing beside her. "Oh, I'm sorry, Peggy, forgive my manners! Margaret Mahoney, I'd like you to meet Paul Franklin, our newest staff member. Paul, this is the Miss Peggy, you've heard so much about."

Paul extended his hand, "I'm delighted to finally meet you, Miss Peggy. I have heard a lot about you. I'm excited to be joining the staff, and I really look forward to working with all of you. Miss Grace and the others have helped bring me up to speed quickly, but I hope to tap into your extensive experience, as well."

"I'm glad to meet you, too, Paul," Peg said as she accepted Paul's handshake. "If your resume is only half true, we are most fortunate to have you as a colleague – and a new friend."

"I'll leave the two of you to get acquainted," Grace said as she walked toward the door. "But please do stop by to see me before you leave, Mrs. Mahoney. Wow! It sure sounds strange to call you that, doesn't it? But I guess you (and I) will have to get used to it!" Paul and Peggy could hear her chuckle as she headed down the hall.

"Please pull a chair off the pile and let's chat a bit if you have the time," Peg suggested, indicating the furniture still piled in the middle of the room.

"I've been looking forward to meeting you…ah…do I call you Margaret, Peg or Miss Peggy? I must admit, I'm a little confused," Paul said.

"Peg is fine," Peggy laughed. "I have to say, we're so pleased that Grace will now be able to return to the classroom part-time. It's great that some of the administrative duties will be on someone else's capable shoulders."

Paul nodded, "I'm looking forward to the shared assignment too. My previous job was a shared assignment, and it worked out quite well for both parties. We felt it was also good for the students…and the school. Grace and I are still trying to sort out the administrative split. I'm sure we'll be able to tweak the job responsibilities as the year progresses. She and I have common philosophies, and our interests and strengths seem to complement one another."

"Grace has really missed working directly with the lower elementary children the last few years, and it'll be a bonus for the children to have a male teacher," Peggy assured him.

"How did you find things in Bergamo?" Paul asked.

"That's right! I'd forgotten that you got your certification there too," Peg said. "It was wonderful! So many dedicated people are on the staff there, and they're always looking for new, creative ways to enhance the core Montessori principles. By the way, how did you happen to study there?"

"I'll make the long story short," Paul began. "I was actually living in Bergamo at the time – sort of a post-college European adventure. I had a job there, but not in education… and I had some time on my hands. A colleague's wife was getting her primary certification at the Center. She invited me to an event there, since she knew that my older sister was a Montessori Directress and I had teaching credentials."

"So you were already familiar with Montessori?" Peg asked.

"Yes," Paul continued. "My original career goals were hopefully going to lead me to becoming a high school teacher, basketball coach, and, perhaps, an administrator."

"How about your parents, are they teachers too?"

"Dad was a high school biology teacher and basketball coach. Mother was primarily a church organist, but she did give piano lessons from time to time. Unfortunately, she passed away last year. Her condition was the main reason I returned to the States, so I could help Dad care for her during the final year of her life. I was fortunate to get a shared teaching/administration job in my home town. It was a blessing to have that time with my dad and mother."

"I'm so sorry about your mother, Paul. I'm sure having you there was a comfort for both your parents," Peg offered. "How's your father doing now?"

"He's begun a new life in Florida sharing a home with his younger brother, who also lost his wife. How about your parents? Did I hear that you grew up on a farm?"

"Yup, I sure did," Peg replied. Mom and Dad still live on the farm where my three brothers and I grew up. My mom is a retired Home Economics – or should I say Family Living – high school teacher. Dad has a degree in Ag Education but never taught. He loves farming and also serves on the County Commission. My youngest brother is now in vet school at MSU, another is an attorney and the oldest is a farm management consultant."

"Three brothers? That must have been a lively household. Well, it certainly sounds like your family is doing well. Did they tell me that your husband is a professor on campus?" Paul asked.

"Yes, he's an associate professor in the College of Agriculture and Natural Resources," she explained. "His main interest is in improving the quantity and quality of oil seeds produced by a tropical weed that most people have never heard about." Peggy laughed.

"Hey, that's impressive! Has he been at State for his entire career?"

"No," Peggy continued. "Actually, he only came to MSU last year. Before that he was at Texas A & M. He did live here as a child when his dad was on the faculty, though. I know he'll look forward to meeting you. He likes interacting with people who have other interests than his…and he's pretty knowledgeable about Montessori, now that he's visited the Bergamo Center, himself."

"By the way, have you found a place to live, yet? I know the area pretty well, having lived here for the last five years."

"Yes, thanks. I'm all set for now. I'm renting a furnished apartment close to the school." Paul went on, "I plan to check out the area and eventually find a place where I can build. Building my own house is something I've had in the back of my mind for some time."

"That sounds pretty challenging. So, you also have construction skills, too…that's good to know!" Peggy said thoughtfully. "Ian and I live in what was Ian's home in Okemos when he was a youngster…and…he was actually a student at Ojibwa! We'll have to have you over for dinner, once I get organized. Ian lost his wife while in Texas, so he… rather WE have a pair of five-year-old twins, Michael and Mia. They attend school here, so you'll get to know them, soon, as well."

"Thanks, I'll look forward to meeting them…and Ian, too. I'm pretty excited about becoming part of this community and learning about life in the mid-west." Paul said, standing. "Thanks for taking the time to fill me in, Peg. I certainly appreciate how welcoming everyone has been. Don't work too hard," he added pointing to the pile of furniture still waiting for Peg to tackle. "I'll see you soon."

"Hmmm," Peg thought to herself, "having a man on the staff will be a good thing for Ojibwa staff, gender, as well as ethnic diversity can only be a positive for our students."

After a pleasant but exhausting day, Peg collected the twins, and the trio set out for home. Peg was glad that Ida, who was continuing to work part-time for the family, was back from Colorado and had left a meal ready for her to pop in the oven.

Over dinner the twins chattered on about their successful shift in the market. "People really liked our cherry tomatoes," reported Michael, "and our beans, onions and peas!"

"And I sold all the little soaps and packages of tea we made," chimed in Mia. "Someone bought the basket I made, too…in fact, we sold everything we had!"

"We made lots of money for the greenhouse," added Michael, "and I got to make change for people."

"It was fun…just like playing store…but it was a REAL store!!" Mia said excitedly.

"It sure sounds like fun," their dad smiled. "Did your mom buy anything?"

"Yup!" Michael said proudly, "where do you think these tomatoes came from? Their OURS!"

"And you'll get to use some of our soap, Daddy. Mommy bought that, too!" Mia interjected.

Their dad laughed, "Well, I'm certainly proud of you both…and I'm glad to hear that you're able to earn money. Does that mean it's time for you to get a job?"

"Daddy!!!!!" the twins squealed simultaneously.

"Hey, Daddy, tell us about your day," Mia changed the subject. "When can we go to your office? Do you need us to help you, again?"

"I'd love for you to come and help me, sometime. Perhaps before school starts," Ian promised.

"Okay, Daddy," Michael answered. "We're done eating, can we be excused and go outside to play? I want to see if Libby is out there, so we can tell her about the market."

"Sure, go ahead," their dad replied. "We'll call you when it's time to come in."

"See ya!" yelled Mia as she and her brother raced to the back door.

The adults shook their heads and laughed…then continued their conversation.

"So, did you see anyone up in your office today, Ian?" Peg asked.

"Several of the guys in my department stopped by to set up a meeting about their program and the trip to Mozambique. I'm sure you remember Kevin and Jay."

"Of course," she said. "I know you're glad to see that things are moving along on the program you helped them initiate."

"True," he confirmed, "and now, after that rocky start last year, they're not only colleagues…but friends as well. But the big surprise was a visit from a former Texas A & M grad student who's now an MSU faculty member."

"Really? In your department?" Peg asked.

"No, she's in the Horticulture Department," he said. "She was an excellent student, so she'll be a good addition to the faculty."

"What a small world. Let's forget about the dishes and grab this moment for some grown-up conversation," Peg suggested.

"Good idea…anything to delay the dishes!" Ian agreed as they moved to the couch in the living room. "Jordan Taylor was a very bright, thoughtful master's student in my research course a couple of years ago. I didn't have many women in the class that term, so she sort of stood out."

"Was she popular with the male students in the class?" Peg wanted to know. "I imagine it can be tough being a rare female in a largely male major."

"Not especially popular," he remembered, "she was actually pretty stand-offish. She was quite tall and tended to wear baggy sweat clothes. She had a long braid down her back and was quite plain, as I recall."

"I can see how she might have differed from other coeds,"

Peg offered.

"To tell you the truth, Peg, it was so soon after Laurie died that I didn't pay much attention to any women...colleagues or students. I had too much on my mind, then, to do anything except focus on being the best dad and teacher I could be. But I did appreciate Jordan's curiosity and zest for learning. It's not often that you get somebody who is so obsessed with squeezing every detail possible out of a lecture. I honestly didn't recognize her today when she walked into my office. She looked like a completely different person."

"You lost contact with her after that class?" Peggy wanted to know.

"Well, the following year she asked me to supervise her special independent study project. She was interested in modifying a variety of ornamental grass. I lost track of her when she began her doctorate." Ian explained.

"Were you surprised to learn that she was at State?"

"Yes and no. Last year, I was asked informally by the chair of the search committee for a recommendation of sorts when she applied for the position here. He knew I was from A & M and thought I might know her. I remember telling him that she was one of the brightest students I ever had. But it was a passing thing that I subsequently forgot. I was in Africa, I think, when she came for an interview. Let's face it...the past few months I've had my mind on other things – such as proposing to and marrying YOU!"

Peggy laughed, "What a sweet thing to say! I must sound like a jealous wife! I actually look forward to meeting her... perhaps I can find out what you were REALLY like in your old life. Let's invite her for dinner soon."

"I already suggested that to her, but I have to warn you, she still doesn't seem like a very sociable person. She certainly looks different...very professional and confident...

not at all like the young girl that was in my class."

"Now I am eager to meet her," Peg said, warming to the challenge of getting to know this mystery woman. "We'll have to introduce her to that new group for young singles at church."

"Good idea. So, how was your day?" Ian asked, changing the subject.

"It was a great surprise to walk into my freshly-painted classroom. It looks great!" Peg bubbled. "Then Grace stopped by to welcome me back and introduce our new staff member, Paul Franklin. He's the new Montessori Director who will be splitting classroom and administrative duties with Grace."

Ian scratched his chin, thoughtfully, "Wasn't he the guy who came for an interview while you were at the farm? I think I remember you saying his resume was impressive."

"The same one," Peg affirmed. "Did you know he was also certified at the Center in Bergamo?"

"Really? That's pretty amazing! How did that happen?" Ian asked.

"I'm not exactly sure," Peg explained, "but he was there working some other job and decided to get certified in his spare time. He has a sister who is a Directress, so he was familiar with Montessori. He told me that he'd trained to be a high school teacher and perhaps a coach like his father… but had also been interested in administration."

"Do you think he might have been playing basketball in Europe?" her husband suggested.

"He is tall enough to have been a player, and his dad was a coach, but he didn't mention anything about being involved in sports," Peg said.

"You know, his mother was a church organist, so maybe he sings and could join our church choir…or maybe he could be a candidate for Pastor Becky's young singles group, too…like Jordan!"

"Wouldn't hurt to ask and invite him to participate in both," Peg agreed.

Peg and Ian headed to the back door to call in the children. After bedtime routines, tucking the twins into bed, and finishing the now-dried, food-caked dishes…Peg and Ian collapsed onto the sofa and reached for each other's hands.

"Oh, Peggy," Ian began holding her hand and kissing it softly, "being able to share my day at the office with you is so special for me. I hope you know how often I thank the good Lord that you came into my life. The children and I are surely blessed to have you for our wife and mother."

"It's my prayer of thanks to be part of this family, as well," Peg agreed, leaning over and kissing him gently. "And, yes, we are all truly blessed!"

So ended another day on Ottawa Drive.

CHAPTER FOUR

"What an interesting day," thought Jordan, as she quickly changed into shorts and a loose t-shirt after arriving at her home. Since there was a nice evening breeze, she looked forward to enjoying a bit of quiet time on her deck. The first days at the office had really been busy, but she was determined get things organized properly before classes began.

"Hello there, neighbor," called out Martha Webb, who was sitting in a lounge chair on her adjacent deck. "You must have had a long day!"

"Hi, back! You must be Mrs. Webb. Your son, George, told me you were in the adjoining apartment," Jordan said walking over to Martha and offering her hand. "I'm pleased to meet you. I'm Jordan Taylor…and, yes, it was a long day," she laughed as she tucked a lock of damp hair behind her ear and fanned her perspiring face. "Does it really show that much? It took me longer to organize my office and set up the lab than I expected."

Jordan dropped into her cushioned deck chair with a huge sigh. "I do feel great now that it's done, though. So, Mrs. Webb…tell me about you? I only know that you're a great mom, because your son is delightful! He was certainly looking forward to starting that sabbatical in England. I've really been looking forward to meeting you, too, ever since I moved in."

"Please call me Martha," she smiled back, pleased by the comment about her son. "I just got back yesterday afternoon after spending a few days at a friend's cottage on Lake Michigan. It's so hot and humid here this week, that after a quick trip to the farmers' market, I decided to spend the rest of the day reading and relaxing. Hey, have you even had any dinner yet? I have some chicken salad left in the frig, if you're interested."

"Why, thanks, Martha. That's very sweet of you," Jordan said, taken aback by the friendly offer from someone she'd just met, "but I stopped at Taco Bell on my way home and got a big taco salad."

"How about a piece of peach cobbler?" Martha persisted. "I made it fresh after I came from the market…then I ate so much chicken salad, I couldn't add another bite. But now… I'd be happy to have a piece with you. It's an old family recipe…and I even have some Reddi-whip, to top it off."

"That sounds wonderful," Jordan said, her mouth watering at the thought. "I have some iced tea in the refrigerator, so let me grab a couple of glasses for us."

"That would be great," Martha said as she opened the sliding door into her kitchen. "I'll come over and join you at the table on your deck."

The two sat across from each other and enjoyed this unexpected meeting and chance to get acquainted.

"I'm so glad you moved in next door," said the older woman. "George and Susan offered to have me stay in their house…but I really prefer my little attached apartment. It's just perfect for me. I hope, however, that you don't think I'm an old busy-body who'll barge in on you, be nosey about your business and always be asking favors of you. That's really not my style. I may be 80 years old, but I'm very busy with my own life."

Jordan laughed, she liked this forthright woman, immediately. "Goodness, no. I'm delighted that you're right next door and hope to pick your brain about what's going on in the community. I really don't know anyone in Michigan, since I just moved here from Texas. I only know one former professor that I had at Texas A & M and the committee members who interviewed me when I came in January."

"I'm sure you'll get acquainted quickly, Jordan. There are a lot of young professionals in the area," Martha assured her.

"Maybe…but I'm not really a 'joiner.'" Jordan found herself confiding. "I don't plan to get into a bunch of organizations or clubs just to meet people. I'm actually pretty uncomfortable walking into a room full of strangers. Besides, I plan to immerse myself in my career, and I'm definitely not interested in dating!" Jordan added, perhaps a little too forcefully.

Martha nodded, wondering why this attractive young woman was so adamant about avoiding people her own age. Surprisingly, Jordan answered that question without being asked.

"I've always been too busy to do much socializing. Ever since I was a teenager, I've always been in school and working. In the summers before I went to college, I worked at a landscaping company…trimming, weeding, planting, watering, hauling dirt. Then, in college I always had part-time jobs, internships, whatever I could get to help with the college and graduate school expenses. I guess I was too busy to get attached to other people…and I especially avoided any romantic entanglements," Jordan said defiantly with her chin raised slightly.

"You, know, Jordan," Martha said, laying her hand reassuringly on Jordan's arm. "I sense that maybe you feel like you have to explain why you are who you are. It's really not necessary. I can tell already that you're the type of person who takes relationships seriously. You're certainly light-hearted and open. Just know, we're all reluctant to do things that make us feel uncomfortable...that's just normal, my dear."

Jordan swallowed...she found she had an unexpected lump in her throat. How could this old woman, who she'd just met, see inside her so clearly. In some strange way, amazingly, this woman reminded her of her father. Her dad used to talk to her like this. It was like he could see inside her soul...and he understood. Suddenly, she missed him very much.

Jordan said quietly, eyes down, "Martha...I don't exactly understand this...but...you remind me of my dad, who I loved very much."

"Loved?" Martha repeated.

"My dad died several years ago in a tragic accident. He used to say the same things to me that you just said. It's almost like I heard...him speaking to me." Jordan said, her voice cracking.

"Oh, my dear girl," Martha said comfortingly as she rounded the table, took Jordan's chin, raised it gently, and peered deeply into her eyes. "Of course, you still miss him. The hurt of losing someone you love never really goes away. The words I said are words that are in your heart. Your father could see the open, fun-loving, engaging person you are. Perhaps when you lost him...you somehow lost the person he saw in you."

Tears streamed unchecked down Jordan's face. "Oh, Martha," she said, "I can't explain this crazy feeling I have about you. I feel like I have known you forever...and we just met! How can that be?"

Martha pulled a tissue from her pocket and handed it

to Jordan. She sat beside her, put her arm around Jordan's shoulder, and pulled her close. "I've lived a long life, my dear. I've met a lot of people...I've lost a lot of friends and family members, too. But there's one thing I have learned. When the good Lord above hands us an unexpected gift...we need to just accept it...not to question it. I, for one, feel blessed that you moved in next door, and I know, already, that we are destined to become dear friends."

Jordan buried her head in her new friend's shoulder. "I...I never had a grandma, Martha. Grandmas, I know, love you no matter what! It's one of my greatest sorrows. Do you think...would you...? I mean, would it be too much to ask, if you would consider being sort of...a...a substitute grandma...someone who would accept me as I am...warts and all?"

"Why, Dr. Jordan Taylor," Martha said, pushing back and holding Jordan at arm's length, her infectious laugh bursting from deep inside, "that's the best proposition I've had all day!"

Jordan laughed, too, relaxing at last as Martha continued, "I'd be honored to be your grandma. I've had quite a few nephews but no nieces. With only one son, his wife has sort of become my substitute niece and daughter, as well as my daughter-in-law. She's a dear person, and I already miss her. And, of course, there are no grandchildren yet."

"I know you're very busy, Martha...George said that you volunteer at several different places. Is that right?" Jordan asked.

"Yes, I work several shifts each week at the gift shop at Sparrow, the local hospital; and I fill in, as needed, at the Wharton Center Gift Shop. The Wharton Center is the university theater that features Broadway shows, which is nice because I get to see a lot of great shows for free."

"I imagine you have lots of friends," Jordan continued. "If you don't mind my asking, did you have a career or were you a stay-at-home mom?"

"Both my husband and I attended a state teachers' college in Ohio," Martha explained. "He was in English, and I studied to become a business education teacher. We both went to graduate school, which was pretty unusual in those days. But there, I changed my focus and became a librarian. I guess it was natural for George to become a Shakespearean scholar. As you can imagine, there was always a lot of reading in our house."

"It's wonderful that George and Susan can spend the year in England," Jordan added. "I've always wanted to visit Oxford and Cambridge."

"Then I certainly hope that it stays on your 'bucket list' until you do it! I think I remember that George said you grew up in Indiana. Does your mother still live there?"

"Yes, I'm a Hoosier," Jordan confirmed. "We lived in a small town outside of Indianapolis. I have a brother, Bill, who's a basketball coach. Dad was a State Patrol Officer. It was a rainy night while on duty helping a stranded motorist, that he was killed by a hit-and-run driver. It was a shock. We were totally unprepared. That was the main reason my sophomore year in college was so miserable."

"I'm so sorry about your father," Martha soothed. "It must have been doubly hard to lose him when he was being a good Samaritan…and you were so young for such a tragedy."

Jordan got a steely look in her eye as she admitted, "It really made me question all my religious beliefs. How could God allow such a thing to happen? My dad was such a good man! The whole thing made me doubt church, God, even the reasons for trying to live a Christian life. To make matters worse, later that same year, I had a serious accident and could no longer play basketball."

"You played basketball at college?" asked Martha, impressed.

"Actually, I had a full-ride scholarship to play at Purdue. It was a real thrill since the Boilermakers have such strong competitive women's teams. The bonus was that Purdue also had an excellent Ag School, and I was majoring in horticulture. The accident was yet another huge blow to my previously-charmed existence."

Martha's hand covered her mouth in disbelief as she shook her head, sadly, "Oh, my dear Jordan, I'm so sorry! Was it a knee injury? I know that's so common for basketball players."

Jordan shook her head affirming Martha's suspicion, "Yes, I took a nasty fall after a rebound and wrecked my ACL. Although the surgery went well, and I had excellent rehab therapy; my knee was never strong enough to play again…at least not at that level."

"How sad to be forced to give up an activity in which you excelled!" Martha sympathized.

"I confess I didn't handle that or Dad's death very well. You might say that I crawled into my personal shell. Except for studying…which somehow allowed me to forget about the real world…I withdrew from everything I cared about. I ignored my friends, most of whom were basketball players. I put on a lot of weight, wore sweats and avoided human contact as much as I could. But…I was determined to make a name for myself as a research scientist!" Jordan paused from her unintended confession. "I can't believe I'm unloading all of this on you, Mrs. Webb…er…Martha. I…I've never done anything like this before."

Martha again, patted Jordan's arm and chuckled, "That's

what grandmas do, young lady. They listen, they understand, they're there when you feel the need to unload. Another thing they do is appreciate the gift you offer...the gift of yourself. I'm honored that you feel you're able to share so much of yourself with me. But I must say, I certainly don't see that young, lost, overweight, disheveled girl you describe sitting with me on the patio today. Something must have changed along the way."

Jordan laughed, "That's certainly sweet of you to say, but that girl is still inside of me. Right now, I'm only focused on becoming the best research professor I can be. I do hope to be able to connect with students, as well. I have a soft spot in my heart for those that might be struggling the way I did," Jordan admitted. "You know, Martha, talking with you has made me feel so…so, I don't know…so free, in a way. You are like a ray of light in my dim personal life." Laughing, she added, "If I believed in angels…I'd have to say you were sent to me from up above!"

Embarrassed by Jordan's admission, Martha changed the subject, "So, Jordan," she said, "you didn't say, is your mother still living in Indiana?"

"No, she moved on with her life and is working in Arizona. I'll tell you about that another time. She and I were once quite close but not anymore. I was not much help to her after Dad's death. And my brother had just gotten married and moved away. I was away at college, focusing on basketball as a diversion, and too upset myself to even think… or for that matter care…about helping anyone else, even my mother."

Martha paused, then said quietly, "Grieving is difficult for everyone. We all go through the process in our own way. It takes longer for some of us. Although people are trying to be kind when they say, 'I know what you're going through,' they really don't. I hated it when people said that to me… even good friends."

"Mother and I were never again close after Dad was gone," Jordan said with grim acceptance.

"That's so sad! I hope that can change over time," her new friend offered.

"Hard to say," Jordan said sadly. "I took a philosophy of religion course at school in hopes that it might help me, but it really didn't. It did spark some interesting conversations…no, more like arguments…with a classmate. But, as it turned out, those discussions were way more helpful to him than to me."

"You know, Jordan," Martha said, hesitantly, "one thing you said concerns me, I must admit. You said that you were not able to 'help' your mother when she lost her husband. You seem to have shouldered a burden of guilt about not being there for her. Jordan, one day you will be a mother, yourself. When that day comes, you will understand…but in the meantime, you must believe me. It is not the job of a child to comfort and help a parent deal with grief. It is the job of a mother to comfort her child and help her child deal with losing a father. I say this…not to criticize your mother. Clearly, she was in shock and struggling with many things at the time. Rather, I say this because it's important for you to allow yourself to let go of the burden of guilt you have carried for way too long."

Jordan's eyes widened, filled with tears, and she grabbed Martha and hugged her with all her might. "Oh, dear Martha," she sobbed. "Oh, dear, dear, Martha! I've never thought of the situation like that!! I've always blamed myself for my mom's struggles…but, intuitively, I think you might be right. And now, suddenly…I only feel sad for my mom…and for myself… This is too much to contemplate right now…my head, and my heart, are reeling. I don't even know what to say to you…"

"Please don't say anything, my dear," Martha said, pulling back, and patting Jordan's shoulder. "Just take the time to think about it…and try to begin being gentle with yourself. You are a good person with a dear heart, but God's will is not your responsibility."

"Okay, Miss Martha," Jordan said. "I will think about it… but maybe…just maybe…you are, indeed, that angel sent from above!"

Martha laughed, "Well, while I still have my wings… maybe now is the time to say 'Good Night' and get some sleep."

"That sounds like a good idea for both of us," Jordan agreed, "but I have a lot to think about, so I'm not sure how much sleep I'm going to get."

"Jordan, I have this feeling that tonight is the beginning of a wonderful friendship, one that has a special place in each of our lives," Martha said, hugging Jordan one more time. "Good night, my sweet Granddaughter."

"Good night, Grandma, dear" the young woman responded hugging her back.

Settling into her bed that night, Jordan reflected on the magical evening that had just unfolded. How could it be that…like a ray of sunshine from behind a cloud…Martha had entered her life and changed everything. She had so much to think about…so much to forgive…so much to do. Tonight was a catharsis…a new beginning, and she, Dr. Jordan Taylor, had the little old lady next door to thank for this wonderful gift!

CHAPTER FIVE

An exhausted Montessori director dropped his backpack and hastened to grab the phone before it stopped ringing. The bike ride home had left him breathing heavily and damp from the heat and humidity. "I wonder who that is" he thought as he responded, "Hello, Paul Franklin here."

"Hello, Paul Franklin, this is your big sister, Amy! I haven't heard from you since you got to Michigan, and I've been wondering about how things are going. Fill me in, please!"

"Sorry not to have called sooner, Sis, but it's been pretty hectic around here. I spent most of Saturday, scouting the area for food, cleaning supplies and stuff. I'd forgotten how much you need just to get started."

"You got spoiled living with Dad the past two years, Paul. What you need is a wife! I can't believe I just said that," she laughed.

"Yeah, like you've been the 'let me take care of you, dear,' wife for the past ten years! But, seriously…you have to stop worrying about my sex life!" Paul admonished cheerfully. He loved his sister, and actually liked it when she worried about him…up to a point.

"The anniversary bouquet you sent was really lovely, Paulie. It sure is hard to believe it's been ten years, already. Jeff and I were very touched by your thoughtfulness. Many thanks," his sister said, sincerely.

"So, how's Jeff doing? Probably busy as ever. You'll have to tell him he still owes me a rematch on the one-on-one, he took me for last time. Of course, it wasn't really fair, since I had a gimpy ankle!" whined Paul.

Amy laughed heartily, "I'll tell him, but be prepared, he's been shooting hoops in the driveway ever since you left, and he's getting pretty good at his jump shot! Now, tell me about your place, I'm dying to hear the details."

"First of all, it's been great not to have to furnish it. The apartment is comfortable and not far from the school. In fact, I had just biked home, when you called. Although, I have to admit, it was way too hot and humid to bike today...I'm drenched with sweat!" he exclaimed, mopping his face with the tail of his shirt.

"Oooh, gross..., little bro..." Amy interrupted.

"Yeah, I probably should have driven today...but it's great being close. And another good thing about renting this place for the first nine months, is that I'll have plenty of time to check out the area to find a place to build," Paul added.

"You've always said you wanted to build your own place, so you're thinking now might be the time?" Amy asked.

"Well, we'll see. This just may be the place, but the good thing is...I have some time to find out," Paul answered.

"So, tell me about the school. Is it like ours, here in Virginia?" Amy was anxious to know.

"No, it's actually even nicer...all in one building on a beautiful, wooded lot. The original architect must have been a genius. He captured the essence of what a Montessori School should be like...lots of open space with doors opening to play yards for each classroom. They've been able to expand the facility several times without destroying the original design. There's even a full-sized gym and a greenhouse. Maria Montessori would have loved it!"

"I'm so jealous!" Amy complained. "Having classes in different locations makes it hard to think of us as a single school community. I forgot if you told me, but how many children are enrolled in your school?"

"Right now, there are less than 150. According to their strategic plan, though, they'd like to have at least 170," he admitted. "But you know how it is…the elementary classes are still growing, but there's a long waiting list for the primary classes. I'll send you pictures next week of the classrooms, the greenhouse and the grounds. There's even a wetland area as part of the property."

"Oh, good…do that, Paul. I'm anxious to see Ojibwa. I'd love to come and see the place for myself, sometime," Amy said. "So, what do you think about the rest of the staff? Have you met everyone yet? I think you told me that several people were gone this summer, when you went for your interview."

"Hey, Ames, I'd love to have you and Jeff come for a visit!" he responded enthusiastically. "Yes, you're right about the staff…several were gone this summer, but most seem to be back in town, now, eager to set up their classrooms and get ready for the new school year. Just like at your school, only a few of the directresses are involved in the summer sessions. But of those I've met, they seem to be quite a diverse group. One of the older women is from India, and there's another young African American woman…both are sharp, energetic and eager for school to start. Looking over some pictures of the school's history, it appears that diversity has always been one of their goals. Grace, the woman I'm job-sharing with, is about 50 and from everything I can tell so far, she's going to be a great teammate and mentor!"

"Are there any other men on board?" Amy asked.

"Nope...I'm numero uno," he chuckled. "But, there are a couple of interesting guys on the board, and several of the dads are active in the parents' group. One of the custodians is male, as is the groundskeeper. Years ago, they had another male director, who was trained in Italy. He was involved in starting the expanded elementary program but didn't stay very long. You know...like I've always said, Ames, 'a good man is hard to find!'" He laughed.

Amy grimaced, "Puleeeez, Paul!"

"Actually, I've been told that from time to time they've had men come in to lead special foreign language programs," he went on. "One was a professor from the Lansing Community College, who taught the children Mandarin Chinese. Last year a fellow did some enrichment classes in Spanish conversation. I noticed in the strategic plan that there's interest in establishing an across-the-board foreign language program...one that's committed to being around for at least four or five years."

"Having both genders is certainly a positive in my book," Amy commented. "Likewise, making a commitment to fund a foreign language program is also a good thing. We do live in a global society and the more we can prepare our kids for a diverse world...the better. I wish our board was more willing to do that kind of planning."

"Today I spent some time with one of the women I hadn't met before. Her name is Margaret Mahoney...Peg, and she is the directress who also trained in Bergamo. This will be her sixth year as a primary teacher here at Ojibwa. She actually worked here part-time as an aide when she was an undergrad. She just returned from her honeymoon. I already know that I'll be able to count on her to help me transition into the Ojibwa learning community."

"I expect that the two of you had lots to talk about. Was

she surprised at how you came to get certified in Italy?" Amy wanted to know.

"Well, we never actually got around to talking about that, except that I did mention you and your Montessori connection," Paul told her. "As I said, she'd worked at Ojibwa part-time as a student, and the Board was so impressed with her, they offered her a fellowship to get certified. She had to agree to come back to the school for at least five years, which she readily did. Then, she opted to study in Italy…perhaps because she wasn't able to go on a study abroad experience when she was younger."

"Is she local?" Amy probed.

"It must feel that way after spending a decade in the Okemos area, but I think she grew up on a farm not that far from here. Everyone in her family graduated from MSU," he explained. "I guess I'll have to get a Michigan map and begin learning about this state, won't I?"

"Good idea!" Amy answered, but quickly got back to Peg. "So, what does her husband do? Is he in education too?"

"Aren't you the curious one? He's a professor at the university but grew up in Okemos. He even attended this school as a youngster. I'm not sure exactly what his field is…something to do with plants, I think. At lunch, I heard two of the women talking about him doing work in Africa. I don't know what that's all about."

"He should be an interesting guy for you to get to know," Amy said, continuing to worry about her brother's social life. "Is he into sports? How old is he? I hope you meet a couple of men you can hang out with."

Paul let out a belly laugh, "Oh, Ames…you'll never change! You are so nosey and always ask way too many questions! Too bad you didn't decide to become a lawyer! I do know a lot about him, though. His name is Ian and he's fairly new on campus. He was married before, a widower with a pair of twins who are enrolled in our school. Miss Peggy, as the children call her, was their directress. That's how the two met."

"Are there any single women on the staff?" Amy badgered him.

"Amy!!!! You are incorrigible! And…no…not any single directresses, at any rate. I know you mean well, but PLEASE forget it. When the time is right, I'll find my own Mrs. Franklin, thank you very much!"

"Amy smiled to herself, knowing that his plea would not sway her…then in a wheedling voice she said, "Oh, baby bro…I'm only looking out for your best interests!"

Shaking his head, Paul had to admit, "Amy, I really do want to find a soulmate…just as you did, but finding someone like you and Mom is just not that easy. And I'm getting to be even more picky, the older I get. Finding a woman who is fun, caring, not too smart for a dumb 'jock' like me and a Christian…isn't someone who's standing on every street corner waiting for me to come along."

"No wonder you're still a bachelor!" Amy said, exasperated. "Forget finding Ms. Perfect…you'll never find someone like me, after all…just find someone that is breathing and can put up with you…that's enough for me!"

Amy took an exaggerated breath, "I guess I'll just have to keep praying!"

Again, Paul shook his head in equal parts disbelief and appreciation for the sister who cared so much about him. "Thanks, Sis, do that. In the meantime, I plan to find a church home. There are plenty of choices, and I heard that there's a new singles group for young…whatever that means…professionals in an interfaith chapel in Okemos. I like the sound of being part of a chapel, which to me connotes a small congregation, where it may be easier to get involved. I might even decide to join the choir if they have one."

"That would please Mother," Amy voiced her approval. "Most church choirs are short on tenors, especially those who sing with gusto! As you remember…Jeff and I met in a singles group twelve years ago…and look what happened to us! Let's hope the Franklin romantic good fortune continues…"

"You never can tell," he gave up the fight.

"Do you have plans for tonight?" Amy wanted to know.

"Not really," he admitted. "While not tough physically, it has been an exhausting week. You know, I have to admit, learning all those names, school policies, my long list of administrative tasks…has been more tiring than I expected. In a way, this is my first real job. The two years at home were always 'temporary' in my mind."

"I hadn't thought of it that way, but I suppose you're right," Amy agreed. "Although playing basketball in Europe was a fulltime job for a couple of years, it wasn't where you expected to make your mark professionally, so, I guess it can be thought of as being temporary, too."

"Yeah," he nodded, "and maybe because I was self-aware enough to know that the NBA was not in my future, playing in Europe seemed more like an encore to college ball than a serious career option."

"Hey, guy, it's been good talking with you," Amy, realizing the time, started to end the call. "I'll give Dad a call and fill him in on your move to Michigan."

"Thanks, again for calling, Ames," Paul said, sincerely. "It's a bit lonely here. I haven't even had time to meet my next-door neighbors, and I miss having conversations with Dad in the evenings."

"Yeah, I'll bet he misses them, too. You might just give

him a call yourself!" Amy couldn't stop herself from advising. "I'd better hang up now and let you get a bite to eat. Do stay in touch, little bro. I miss you!"

"Will do, Sis," Paul responded warmly. "Thanks for always being in my corner. Love you lots!"

"Love you back!"

"Now for a shower and some dinner," he thought. "I'm sure glad I like to cook. Tonight, it'll be stir fry and a couple of those nice tomatoes and ripe peaches I picked up the other day."

Then whistling a jaunty tune, he headed for the shower, before getting busy in the kitchen. "Yes," he said aloud, "coming here now was the right move. With God's help and my hard work, I think that this just might be the perfect place for me…I guess we'll see."

CHAPTER SIX

As the family was leaving for their day's activities, Ian commented to his wife, "Hey, My Dear, I forgot to mention that my afternoon meeting today was cancelled, so I called the school to schedule a time to observe the twin's class. I'm anxious to see how this year's class differs from last year's primary class."

"How nice," Peg responded. "I'm so glad you'll be able to do an observation before our first parental conference. You might not notice too much change, though, because we try to make the transition gradual. The really noticeable difference comes when they move into the Lower El program. Be sure to stop by my classroom to say, hello, too!"

After eating breakfast, grabbing backpacks and quick kisses good-bye…Peg and the children climbed into her Volt and headed off to school. Ian wondered if the kids would pay any attention to him when he arrived that afternoon to observe. He remembered that when he visited their classroom in the past, it was pretty uneventful. Nobody seemed to pay much attention to him…or any observer, for that matter. Visitors were told to say very little in response to any recognition shown by the children. "Hi, I'm here to watch you work," was to be the observers' only comment before sitting quietly in a corner and watching what was going on. Because there were frequent visitors in the classroom, the children just went about their business and barely noticed the guests in their midst.

That afternoon there were a dozen five-year-olds in the kindergarten classroom. Ian had been told that some four-year-olds might be joining the group for part of the afternoon, so they were there, too. Ian noticed that there was ethnic diversity among the children and that both the teacher aide and directress were international professionals. He was pleased the children were interacting with ethnicities and cultures different from their own.

There were no live animals in the classroom, as there had been last year. The room had an assortment of child-sized tables of different shapes and child-sized chairs. There were two large easels and a stack of rolled-up rugs. Since the school had a large library, the room had no library of its own, but there was a large assortment of picture books as well as easy readers in various places throughout the room. A full set of bells was arranged on its own table.

When Ian entered, he noticed that most of the children seemed to be working in pairs. For the most part, boys worked with boys and girls with girls. Naturally, his attention was drawn to Mike and Mia. Ian's chair was located close to where Mia and her little friend were seated on a small rug using colored markers to draw on a large sheet of chart paper. Beside the paper was a large wooden map puzzle. From what he was able to see, their work looked like a bunch of scribbles…different colored lines, drawn close together. The girls were totally absorbed in their work. Just then, Mia picked up a puzzle piece.

"Do you know what this is?" Mia asked her partner.

Her partner shook her head, "No."

"This," said Mia, the little tutor, "is Africa." Picking up another piece she continued, "This one is Europe. See all of these little shapes inside the big one? They're countries." Mia pointed to the bottom part of the puzzle piece, "…and this one…is Italy. Don't you think it kind of looks like a boot?"

"Yeah," nodded her friend, "it does!"

"My mommy went to school there to learn to be a Montessori Directress. But I don't know the names of all these other countries," Mia said sweeping her hand over the large puzzle piece that was Europe.

"Hey, Mia," her classmate said, "do you want to do oceans now?"

"Sure," Mia agreed, "but let's paint them this time, okay?"

The girls returned the puzzle pieces to its designated box and placed it on the shelf. Then, with great care, they carried their drawing to one of the easels located across the room. After attaching it and donning paint shirts, they each selected a different shade of blue. For the next ten minutes they worked diligently to fill in all the remaining white space with two shades of blue.

Ian leaned forward to inspect the finished work of art. To his amazement…the scribbles and lines had magically become the various continents! The different colors actually replicated the colors of the various continents on the painted wooden puzzle. And the oceans surrounded them all. Ian shook his head in wonder at the creativity he had watched unfold.

At another table, a child was busily working on a drawing of the face of a clock, as he sat facing the classroom wall clock. Periodically, he sketched a smaller clock with hands on it depicting the time. Later when he put his work in his "cubby," Ian noticed that on each sketch, the child had written the time in actual numerals…2:10, 2:15, etc. "Smart kid," Ian thought, amazed.

Two little girls were practicing writing names in cursive. Each wrote her own name; checked it with her co-worker and then wrote the other's name. The girls were learning to write two different first names…in cursive…in kindergarten! They took turns several times. If the names didn't look quite right, they figured out how to fix them. "What a great example of teamwork," the professor said to himself. Before the two ran over to string some beads, replicating patterns, they grinned and gave each other a "high five."

Ian noticed that nobody showed an interest in the bells. He later learned that one of the lads had perfect pitch and often worked with them. In fact, the child had actually composed a little song that he performed for a special program recently.

Ian looked over at his son, Mike. He was sitting at a table across the room working on some kind of math problem. It didn't appear to involve counting a string of beads or assembling a cube of beads, tasks that had been typical in the primary class. Whatever he was doing, involved a small shallow box with items in it. Michael was concentrating very hard and frowning from time-to-time. He appeared to be working on some kind of calculation. Another boy was standing behind Mike and occasionally asking him a question, which Mike always answered patiently, without looking away from his task.

Ian was curious about what he was doing, so he quietly asked the aide. She replied in a whisper that the standing child was observing Mike perform a skill that was new to the other boy. By observing classmates perform new tasks, children learned from each other…even before they had received formal instruction. "Hmmm," thought Ian, "another great example of kids learning from kids." Michael remained at that station for a full half-hour, focusing on that one learning activity...long after the other boy had left.

Later, his son got a rug and a large piece of chart paper and laid both on the floor. Then he selected a wooden box from a shelf, filled it with markers. From another shelf, Mike took the same box of puzzle pieces that Mia and her friend had been working with earlier, and took them both to the rug. Mike took a puzzle piece and began tracing it on the sheet of paper. Then he did another. Ian observed him trace piece after piece, occasionally looking up at the world map posted on the classroom wall. Soon, a map of the world began to take shape on Mike's paper.

Ian was, once again, intrigued, as he watched Mia participate in an activity near the end of the day. The directress sat on the floor, surrounded by four or five children. As they watched carefully, the woman used a tiny rake to smooth out a light covering of sand in a flat box. Then she carefully arranged eight or nine stones on the sand. After the group silently appraised what she had done, different children took turns in repeating the process in different patterns.

As he left the room Ian asked the directress what that activity was all about.

She smiled and said, "Oh, we're making a Zen garden. It's a nice way to relax and have a bit of quiet time before clean up at the end of the day. Sometimes, we read a story or do some other quiet activity."

"Good idea," Ian thought as he picked up an observation form from the office.

Ian completed the form and stopped to introduce himself and chat briefly with another parent who identified herself as Mrs. Angela Wang. She was dressed in loose, Asian-looking pants and flowing top. She smiled and said, "I'm here to demonstrate Tai Chi for the staff, because I'll be teaching an after-school enrichment class starting next week. That's why

I'm dressed this way."

"Tai Chi," said the professor. "I thought that was for old people. I've seen pictures of large groups of elders performing what I thought were Tai Chi moves in parks and other outdoor spaces…in what I think was China."

"Yes," Angela explained, "that often happens in China, but it's also a popular form of exercise in many retirement homes in this country."

"So, you're offering a Tai Chi class here at the school…for the children?" Ian asked, perplexed.

The Tai Chi leader laughed. "I used to have a school in Massachusetts, and I introduced a class called 'Tai Chi for Kids.' It was really quite amazing. After eight or ten weeks of exercises, I saw many positive changes in the children who performed Tai Chi. They appeared to have developed better communication skills, improved behavior, more large muscle flexibility, increased mental focus…all of which seemed to positively impact the children's ability to concentrate and work together. We began an informal research project at the school…some classes used Tai Chi, others did not. We kept careful diagnostic and anecdotal assessments on the children. After two semesters, both the other teachers and the parents were demanding Tai Chi for all children. I'm a firm believer that Tai Chi exercises can result in improved academic performance and creativity. That's why, when my children enrolled here, I offered to provide a trial enrichment series at Ojibwa."

"Wow!" Ian remarked, totally captivated by this fascinating woman. "Where do I sign my children up?"

Angela Wang laughed. "Why don't you talk it over with your wife and children first." She grabbed a brochure from her flowered shoulder bag. "This will give you a simple explanation of Tai Chi. Basically, it's an Eastern exercise that emphasizes wholeness – of the mind, the body and the spirit. By contrast, Western-style exercises are mainly focused on developing the body."

"Thank you, Angela, I'm anxious to read it," Ian said. "My wife's a directress here, Miss Peggy, so I know she'll be interested, as well."

"If you decide to enroll your children," she told him, "the series of ten lessons will begin next Monday. This afternoon, I'm providing the staff with a short demonstration of the things I'll be doing with the children."

"Well, then, Peggy will already be an expert when we talk tonight," Ian smiled, offering Angela his hand and shaking hers warmly. "Thank you so much for the short course on Tai Chi. We'll talk it over and let the school know immediately of our decision. It certainly sounds like something that Mike and Mia would enjoy. And, of course, all the possible benefits are hard to ignore."

"It was a pleasure to meet you, Ian," said Angela, "I'm sure we'll see one another often at the school…regardless of what you decide about the classes."

Ian picked up the children and they went home together. Since Peg had an after-school meeting, he and the children were planning to make dinner.

Ian could hardly wait to tell Peg about his visit to the school. After the twins were down for the night he shared in great detail his observations in the classroom.

"It never ceases to amaze me," he admitted. "The children just go about their chosen tasks oblivious to the adult visitors in the classroom. I might as well have been a stump or vacant chair."

"Well, I know it's tough for you not to be noticed," Peg said in a mock-serious tone, "when Dr. Professor walks into a classroom, you're used to being the center of attention."

"Geez," Ian said, embarrassed, "I'm not THAT narcissistic, I hope!"

Peg cuddled up and put her head on Ian's shoulder. Smiling, she continued, "Oh, dear, of course not! It's just that the children are so accustomed to observers, that it's no big deal for them. I remember after one dad had observed, he said that the classroom was just like an office…everyone busy doing his or her own job. And, of course, that's what we want them to do."

Ian kissed Peggy's head and pulled her close. He appreciated how lucky he was to be able to learn from an expert – his wife – about five-year-olds. Like, how most little ones had a very short attention span, unless they were totally engaged in an activity. He thought about how long his two kindergartners were able to amuse themselves building something with Legos or playing professor when they went with him to his office. Today he noticed how different the visiting four-year-olds were from his own children. Had his two really matured that much this year?

When he asked Peg about it, she reminded him, "You know dear, all children develop in their own time and in their own way. When Michael and Mia were in my room last year, even as primary youngsters, they already had an ability to focus. They didn't really jump from one thing to another. And, you will find that even in their class this year, there will be those that still haven't developed the ability to stay on task for more than a few minutes. That's what makes my job so much fun…and so challenging."

"Well, it certainly takes a special person to work with these little ones…each one of whom is unique." He said squeezing her tightly, "Just one more reason why I'm so proud of you… and so thankful that you are the mother of my children."

Peg lifted her face, and the two kissed gently. "I, Dr. Mahoney," Peg said, softly, "am truly the lucky one."

After a few minutes, Ian sat up and said, "By the way, Peg, I met Angela Wang this afternoon. She's the gal who's offering the Tai Chi enrichment classes. I was really fascinated by what she told me about the program. She said she was meeting with all of you after school. What did you think?"

"Actually," Peg said, "she's also an MD and is knowledgeable about many Eastern non-invasive medical procedures, as well. Let's tell the kids about the Tai Chi and see if it's something they'd like to attend. I'm all for it!"

"Now I'm totally impressed by Angela Wang!" Ian remarked, surprised. "She was a teacher in her own school in Massachusetts…and she's an MD, too?"

"Well, she said that they moved here so she could attend medical school, so the MD is recent," Peg explained. "Her family lived in China, where her father was a doctor, so much of her knowledge was acquired while still living there."

"Pretty impressive," Ian remarked.

Before moving to Michigan, the Mahoney children had attended a Montessori school in Texas. That school had offered a Yoga option, but Ian did not enroll the kids. As toddlers, he felt they were too young to add it to their already-long day. Apparently, Ojibwa had also offered Yoga in the past, but once the instructor left, the classes ended.

"If the twins want to enroll in Tai Chi, I'll sign them up tomorrow," Peg volunteered.

"Mrs. Peggy Mahoney," Ian began. "I have something to admit to you."

Peggy glanced at him, warily, "Uh, oh, here it comes…the truth about your secret life…"

Ian laughed out loud. "You never stop surprising me, my dearest one!"

He started again, "I was just going to say that when I fell

in love with you…I fell in love with your passion for life, your tender caring heart, your love for children and your love for me. Little did I know that I would also be marrying someone wise beyond her years…knowledgeable about everything…and someone who would truly be a parenting partner! Mrs. Mahoney, I love you more and more each and every day we're together."

Without speaking, a tear sliding slowing down her cheek, Peg gently took Ian's hand…and they walked slowly up the stairs to their bed, together.

CHAPTER SEVEN

It was a busy and satisfying week at school for Peg, who was now feeding the kids dinner before sending them off with Libby, while she and Ian hosted Jordan and Paul for dinner. It was a warm fall evening, so Libby Lane and the children were planning a bike ride around the neighborhood and a stop for some outdoor play at the park. The children ran to wash up before meeting Libby.

Peg silently gave thanks for Ida, the part-time nanny/housekeeper, who had been there that day to spruce up the house and prepare a pan of her delicious lasagna. Ian set the dining room table, while Peg finished assembling her tossed salad and put it in the refrigerator. Ian also appreciated Ida, and had relied heavily on her almost from the time he moved to Okemos. The family needed her less this year since the children were in school fulltime, and Peg had joined the family; but they had decided to keep Ida on anyway. All of the Mahoneys considered Ida a member of the family. Days like today underscored her value to them all.

"I hope we did the right thing by inviting Jordan and Paul to dinner at the same time," murmured Peg. "I sure don't want either of them to think we're trying to play matchmaker."

Ian overheard her remark and responded, "Hardly, My Dear. They're about the same age, and I doubt that either has had time to make many new friends beyond work. Getting established in a new community is a fulltime job in itself. Without neighbors like the Lanes and having the twins in school last year, I doubt if I would have made the church connection...or even met you, for that matter."

The children had donned their helmets and were ready to join Libby when the doorbell rang. It was a smiling Jordan, carrying a large assortment of cut flowers...mums to be specific. "Come on in, Jordan, and meet Peg and the twins," welcomed Ian. "I hope you didn't have any trouble finding us."

"Not at all," Jordan said. "I'm delighted to be here. This is a lovely neighborhood."

"Jordan, this is my wife Margaret – Peg or Peggy for short. Peg, this is Jordan Taylor, my former grad student at A & M and now a Spartan colleague."

"I'm so happy to finally meet you, Jordan," Peggy said, gratefully accepting the flowers her guest held out to her. "The mums are beautiful...and one of my favorite flowers! Thanks!"

"They're from my garden. I hope you enjoy them, Peg," Jordan said. "It was so nice of you to invite me for dinner, and I was really looking forward to meeting you, as well. Your husband was an inspiration for me while I was an undergrad at Texas."

Peggy smiled and turned to the children, who were eyeing the newcomer with interest.

"Michael, Mia" she said, "this is Miss Jordan. She's one of Daddy's former students who's now a professor at MSU and works in the same building as he does. She babysat for you once when you were just little guys."

"Hello, Miss Jordan," said Mia, always the first to speak. "Did you really babysit for us in Texas?"

"Were we good when you took care of us?" Michael continued, without a pause.

"First of all," Jordan said, bending down to meet them at eyelevel, "I'm delighted to see you both, again, although I would never have recognized you, I must admit. As a matter of fact, I only saw your sweet sleeping faces, because you slept the entire time I was with you!" She laughed, "I must confess, that was probably a good thing, because I was scared silly that I wouldn't know what to do if you woke up or cried…especially both of you! You see, I really wasn't an experienced sitter. I agreed to help your dad, because he had an emergency, and…" She cupped her hands to whisper to the kids, "he was my favorite professor." She winked.

"I like her, Daddy!" Michael bubbled, turning to his dad. "I hope she comes again!"

"Me, too!" agreed Mia. "See ya later, Miss Jordan!" Turning to her brother, she grabbed his arm and said, "Come on, Mikey, we need to go meet Libby for our bike ride."

Off they headed, picking their bikes up from the lawn, as they went.

"Make sure you listen to Libby," Peg shouted to them as they disappeared around the front hedge. "…and have fun!"

Peg asked Jordan, if she would like some iced tea. When she said yes, Peg disappeared into the kitchen to get them all glasses of tea and to put her flowers in a vase.

"Jordan, as I think I mentioned when we invited you, we've also invited one of Peg's new colleagues at the Montessori school. His name is Paul Franklin, and he has a shared position of director and teacher," Ian said. "Paul has just arrived from a teaching assignment in Virginia. Like you, he's new in town, and I've not met him yet, either. We doubt if he's had a chance to meet many folks outside of the school, so we thought this might be a way for both of you to meet us…and someone else outside of work."

"How nice," Jordan said, a little hesitantly.

Just then, Peg returned with a tray holding three glasses of iced tea and a beautiful vase of mums, all of which she placed on the coffee table.

Jordan continued, "I didn't realize that there were male Montessori teachers." She was wondering what kind of man would want to work every day with young children.

"I wish that I could say that there are lots of them," Peg admitted, "but that wouldn't be true. Paul actually trained to be a high school teacher, administrator and coach – like his dad. He happened to be working in Italy at some other job, when the opportunity arose to receive Montessori training and certification in his free time. He found out that he was very well suited for the job…and, as it turned out…loved working with young kids. The center in Bergamo was the same place where I did my training."

Peg added, "I just got a call from Paul, while I was in the kitchen. He's been delayed because of a last-minute appointment with some parents who wanted to re-enroll their child. I guess the youngster was injured in an accident and had to be home-schooled for awhile. They were very anxious about his return, so Paul didn't want to delay their meeting. I assured him it was perfectly okay and told him to take his time, we all understand completely."

"Yes, of course," Jordan said, although she was a little uncertain about meeting this single male and hoped she wasn't being set up. She hated "blind dates!"

Since neither of the hosts knew that much about Paul… or for that matter, Jordan…Peg had thought it seemed like entertaining them together was a good idea. But looking at Jordan's face, Peg was not so sure. She knew she and Ian would have to keep this light and non-threatening. Just then, the doorbell rang announcing the arrival of their other guest.

"Welcome to our home, Paul," Ian said shaking Paul's hand, "I'm Peg's husband, Ian. Come on in and take a minute to relax. It sounds like you're just coming off a rather tricky parent meeting."

Ian led Paul into the living room, where Peg stood up and welcomed him. "Hi, Paul, welcome!"

Jordan stood, as well and looked up at the newcomer. Jordan was a tall woman, but this man was a good four inches taller than she. "Paul," Peg continued, "this is Jordan Taylor. She's a new faculty member and colleague of Ian's at MSU."

"How do you do," Paul said, shaking Jordan's hand, noting her firm grip. "I'm pleased to meet both you and Ian." Paul smiled warmly, then turned to Peggy. "Here's some fruit salsa I learned to make while in Italy. I hope it's not too spicy."

Peg accepted the gift with thanks and went to the kitchen to bring in some appetizers. In addition to the bruschetta she had prepared with fresh mozzarella and tomatoes…Peg added a basket of tortilla chips and a bowl of Paul's salsa." For a half hour the foursome exchanged stories of how they all came to be in Okemos. Paul noticed the flowers, and Peg explained they had come from Jordan's garden. Jordan demurred praise, saying that she was only tending the gardens at the home she was renting for the year, during the owner's sabbatical in England.

After devouring all the appetizers…and Paul's salsa was definitely a hit…the foursome moved to the dining room… along with the vase of mums. Peg brought in the salad, bread and steaming pan of lasagna.

Ian asked if it would be okay if they all said grace together, since, he, for one, had much to be thankful for (looking directly at his wife, who blushed). Paul and Jordan nodded agreeably, and Ian bowed his head and said a brief prayer of thanks for the new friends they all had the good fortune to meet this night and for the food they were about to eat. Then, they all dived into a crisp salad, warm garlic bread and hot cheesy lasagna. Peg was sure to lavish praise on Ida for preparing it for them.

Peg turned to Jordan and asked her about her name. She wondered if it was a family name.

Jordan chuckled, "You can't imagine how many times I've been asked that question. Jordan is unusual…especially for a girl! Actually, my name would have been Jordan regardless of my gender. It was my grandmother's maiden name. She passed away just before I was born. When I was in elementary school, I hated it, but now I appreciate the fact that it's uncommon…and that I'm named for someone whom my parents loved very much."

Everyone smiled and nodded. What a lovely tribute it was to have someone named after you…and what a great way to always remember a grandparent, they all agreed. The conversation then turned to Paul and his background.

"So, Paul, are you a descendant of Ben Franklin?" Ian asked, in jest.

"Not that I know of, although my family has its roots in Virginia," he answered. "I can't say that I inherited Ben's scientific, inventive, writing or political skills, if I am related to him." He also chuckled good naturedly.

Ian told everyone that he was born in up-state New York, but that he and his parents moved to Michigan when he was a baby.

Peg seemed to be the only true Michigander…having been born and raised there. She told everyone that she'd grown up on a farm in the Saginaw Valley, where her parents still lived.

"Jordan grew up in Indiana, isn't that right?" Ian asked looking to her for confirmation.

Jordan nodded, "Yup, and lived there right through college." Turning to Paul, she asked, "Where did you go to school, Paul? Peg said that you got your degree in education and hoped to teach at the high school level."

"I went to a small, liberal arts college near my home. Few have heard of it, unless they're familiar with division-three basketball teams," Paul explained.

Jordan brightened. "Did you play 'round ball' there?" she asked.

"Yup...that's my story...and hoops is my game. How about you? Where did you get your degree?" he countered.

"I'm a Boilermaker...Big 10 all the way," Jordan said, punching her fist in the air. "But my brother, who's a coach, also played basketball at a division-three school. In his case, it was a city college in central Indiana. I doubt that they met your team, unless both schools did exceptionally well at tournament time in the same year."

Ian laughed and remarked how lucky they both were to have landed at a place where college basketball was pretty important. "Both MSU men and women have quality teams," Ian bragged. "Last year Peg arranged for us, the then-three Mahoneys, to join other Montessori families at a women's game against a big Spartan rival, The Ohio State University."

"How about you?" Paul asked Ian. "Did you play basketball? You certainly have the height."

"'Fraid not. Unlike you and Jordan's brother, I chose swimming and track. But Peg's older brother was a good high school player too. We hope that both of our kids show an interest in team sports. At least Mike promises to be tall enough for basketball. Mia already seems to enjoy tennis, but her thing really is horses, ever since the twins got to name a pair of colts on the Gerber farm last spring."

"Did you hang out with your brother and his friends, Jordan?" Peg wanted to know. "I certainly did, but mostly they had me chase balls. They never thought I was good enough to actually play hoops with them."

"Bill is five years older than I, but since I got to be tall quite early, they did let me play with them. In fact, they even taught me to dribble and how to shoot the three ball," Jordan answered.

This led the others to wonder if the tall young woman had played organized ball, herself. With her height and probable talent, she must have delighted the women's high school coach. But before anyone could ask that question, Jordan looked around at the group, blushed and then admitted, "Before you even ask…yes…I did play in high school."

"If I'm not mistaken," said a knowing Paul, "Purdue has had some pretty good women's teams…some think even better than the men. So…fess up! Did you play college hoops?"

Ian and Peg exchange surprised glances.

Again, Jordan blushed at the attention. "Yes, yes," she admitted, "I did play at Purdue. In fact, I also had a scholarship to play at Stanford, but since my dad wanted to see me play, I opted to stay closer to home and joined the Boilermaker squad. "

That obviously impressed Paul, who had the basketball 'smarts' in the room. Paul knew that acceptance to play both at Stanford and at a Big Ten school was quite an accomplishment.

"I never knew that about you, Jordan," Ian said, completely surprised. All I knew was that you were a very bright, hard-working graduate student. Since the Purdue Ag school is very demanding, I just assumed that you were equally dedicated to your studies, as an undergrad."

"Few people at A & M knew, because I never mentioned it. My last two years in West Lafayette were nothing to brag about – they were too painful for me to talk about back then."

"I'm so sorry," murmured Peg, eager to change the subject.

"Thank you," Jordan gave her an appreciative smile. "Suffice it to say that I suffered a debilitating, career-ending injury my sophomore year, not long after we lost my dad. So, my whole focus changed, and school was all about my studies."

It was probably a torn ACL, which could really change a person's dream, Paul surmised. He had been one of the lucky ones, escaping a major injury. He would likely tell you, if asked, that he was able to stretch his ability to the limit. Some might describe him as "a big fish in a little puddle."

"Did you ever dream of playing pro ball, Paul?" Jordan wanted to know, hoping to shift the focus from herself.

"No, never!" Paul said. "I'm a realist. My skills were never good enough for that level of play."

"Paul," interjected Peg, "I suspect you're being too modest. Nosey me, I have to ask, was playing basketball your reason for being in Italy? I know there was an international team in Bergamo."

Paul turned red, was silent for a moment, and finally confessed that when he had a chance to play semi-pro in Europe, he'd opted to play in Italy, where there seemed to be a better fit than elsewhere. He'd enjoyed being part of the Hawks, who were based in Bergamo.

True to his nature, he joked and said, "I chose the Hawks...mostly because I love Italian food! But getting my Montessori certification while there was the true blessing, since that's what really sparked my professional passion."

"I really missed not doing a study-abroad trip as an undergrad. It was just too pricey," remarked Peg. "That's why I jumped at the chance to do the Montessori training in Italy, when the offer arose."

"With my basketball scholarship, fortunately, I was able to go on a pre-freshman study experience in Africa," Jordan shared. "It was an amazing growth experience for a small-town Indiana girl. I think an international experience is invaluable for anyone…at any age."

"Did you, by any chance, get into Mozambique, Jordan?" Ian inquired. Then he then turned to Paul and explained, "That's where we're doing work on my research project."

"Close, but not there, I'm afraid. Maybe the next time you go, I can tag along and play grad assistant," laughed Professor Taylor. "After all, as I said before, grass and weeds aren't that far apart."

Everyone laughed at Jordan's attempt to become a stowaway on Ian's research trip.

"Say," Paul changed the subject. "Do you happen to know anything about churches in the area?"

Peg and Ian looked at each other and laughed. Peg said, "Funny you should ask, Paul. Ian and I were going to tell you guys about our church…and see if you might be interested in some of the things we're doing there."

"You see, the children and I were most fortunate when we first came here." Ian continued. "Our next-door neighbor, who, by the way…was the first to welcome the children and me to the community…turned out to be the pastor of a small interfaith church in Okemos. Then, the children's teacher," he turned to his wife with a bow, "turned out to belong to the same church. She invited me to work with the high school youth group…and the rest is history!"

Paul was eager to find a church home. Jordan not so much. Peg and Ian explained that there were lots of different churches in the area from which to choose, all with a variety of interesting programs. But both of them liked being part of a small, active, growing congregation. They said that the church is so new, it continues to meet in rented space because the congregation doesn't even own a church building.

"Do you have a choir?" Paul inquired.

"Well, our choir has a lot of fun singing," laughed Peg. "We could certainly use a good bass or tenor! But in all fairness, several of the larger churches in the area are well-known for their excellent music programs."

"I could add gusto, if not great musicianship," replied Paul. "My mother was our church organist for many years, so everyone in the family was drafted into the choir."

"How about you, Jordan," Ian asked, "have you found a church home?"

"No, and I've not really been looking," she said a little defensively. "Church and religion are not really my thing."

"Oh, sorry, Jordan," Ian said, chastened. "I should know better than to assume. Actually, when I came here a year ago, I felt the exact same way." He paused and thought about whether he wanted to reveal a personal side of himself that he did not share often. He decided that this was not the time, so he left his statement hanging.

"No offense taken! "But," Jordan said, looking at her watch, "I just noticed the time. I really must leave. I promised to pick up my neighbor at the Wharton Center. She's without transportation tonight, because she left her car running this afternoon, and it has a dead battery. Her shift in the gift shop ends at intermission, which should be about now, so I'd better get over there. Many thanks for the lovely dinner, Peg. It really was great to meet you…and you, Paul. Goodbye all!" With that, she arose and headed for the door.

"Well, thanks for coming…and for the lovely flowers, Jordan. It was great to meet you," Peg said following her to the front door.

After chiming in with their farewells, and waving briefly from the door, the men and Peg paused and looked at each other. It was Peg who broke the silence and said that she felt bad that their discussion about church had caused Jordan to be uncomfortable, which she obviously was.

"Well, Dear, it was nobody's fault. How could any of us have anticipated her feelings on the subject of church or religion," Ian said, trying to reassure himself as well as Peg. "It was a natural topic of conversation to raise with newcomers in the community."

"For my part, I'm glad to learn about your small church," Paul said appreciatively. "After being exposed to all of those huge and often empty cathedrals in Europe, small and active sounds good to me."

Peggy then told Paul a little more about their involvement in the Okemos Interfaith Chapel. They described Pastor Becky and the high school youth group for which they were advisors. They also told Paul about a new group for young single professionals Pastor Becky was starting. It occurred to her that group might be of interest to him.

"I'm going to look in to it. Why not?" he asked. "My sister and brother-in-law met in such a group a dozen years ago. They recently celebrated their 10th wedding anniversary, and she's been bugging me to find just such a group. Meeting an unattached Christian gal is on my 'to do' list. Where better to do that than in church?"

Ian searched in a kitchen drawer until he found some printed material about church events. He handed it to Paul, and extended an invitation to have him visit this Sunday, if he could. He also invited Paul to join some members of the congregation after the service for brunch. Peg and Ian attended regularly and found it was a good way to "debrief" the sermon and get acquainted with other church members."

"That sound great," agreed Paul. "I'll try to join you and give the Chapel a look. Many thanks for the fine dinner and conversation. I'll have to have you over to my place for an Italian pasta meal sometime soon. It may surprise you, but I really do enjoy spending time in the kitchen." And with that he took his leave.

"My," remarked Peg as they cleared the table and tidied up the dining room and kitchen. "That was a different evening than what I was expecting. How about you?"

"Not quite what I was expecting either," Ian agreed. "There appears to be a lot more going on with Jordan, than I ever knew or suspected. Did you think she was a little cool to Paul all evening?"

Although usually Mrs. Mahoney was very perceptive and could get a good read on other women promptly, this one had her baffled. Maybe Jordan had not dated much or possibly had a relationship that went bad. On the other hand, some women these days really did put a priority on achieving professional success rather than adding an M.R.S. to their names. If asked one year ago, she, herself, would have admitted that she wasn't looking for a husband. Of course, that was before she met and became friends with the professor.

"I'm not so sure," Peg disagreed. "I think Paul turned out to be the opposite of what she suspected. Did you see how animated she became, when she found out he played basketball?"

"Maybe you're right. Well, perhaps there'll be another chance for Jordan and Paul, if that's in God's plan," laughed her husband as he dropped a light kiss on the top of her head. Then they dried their hands on a kitchen towel and headed next door to collect the twins.

Jordan picked Martha up at the Wharton Center. Martha

noticed that her driver was very quiet on the drive home. She even seemed rather annoyed – not at all like the excited young woman who, just a few hours ago, was on her way to dinner with a former professor and his new wife. Unsure how to broach the subject, the older woman innocently asked, "How was the dinner with your professor and his family?"

"Nice!" came the almost too-sharp reply. The children weren't with us very long. His wife was friendly and easy to be around; but there was another guest, one I wasn't expecting."

"I see," Martha prodded, "and who was that?"

"A new hire at the Montessori School where Peg teaches, a former semi-pro basketball player named Paul Franklin," she explained. "Ian said that he'd mentioned someone else would be there, but I sure don't recall him saying anything like that...and I think they may have been trying to hook us up in a subtle way."

"And that bothered you?" Martha asked.

"I'm not interested in dating and finding a man!" Jordan said vehemently. "But that wasn't all that made me uncomfortable."

"What else happened?"

"They offered to help us find a church home – certainly not one of my priorities! I have absolutely no interest in joining a church or participating in any church activities!" she said emphatically.

The older woman couldn't help but wonder what had been the hosts reaction to Jordan's discomfiture. She also wondered what she might have said or asked in a similar situation with newcomers. She, as an active church goer herself, would probably have done the same thing – invited the guests to visit her church and explore other religious options in the community. So Martha said nothing.

Jordan plowed on, "I think they were all somewhat embarrassed that they had barged into my space." Noticing Martha's questioning glance, Jordan said. "Well, they were very nice people, and probably felt bad that they could have offended me. I excused myself almost immediately, glad that I had a good reason to leave right then to meet you."

"I'm sorry that the evening ended like that for you, my dear, and hope that maybe sometime you can get together with the Mahoneys…without Mr. Basketball being present," Martha suggested.

As they pulled into the driveway, the older woman thought about what could possibly be behind Jordan's strong resistance to church or even a casual friendship with an eligible young man. She also wondered what she might do to help this clearly-troubled young woman find peace. It was something she would pray about tonight…and begin thinking about tomorrow.

CHAPTER EIGHT

After a hasty evening meal, the four Mahoneys set off for the Okemos Interfaith Chapel. Church members had been called to a special meeting which included volunteers and guests from other congregations interested in partnering with African churches. Pastor Becky had arranged for a creative playtime for children, led by her daughter, Libby, and several other responsible teens.

All comers were greeted by Christian Rosario, Ian's graduate student, who had become quite involved in several of the chapel's new programs. Chris registered everyone, handed out name tags and offered coffee while they waited for the meeting to begin.

According to the agenda that had been circulated, the first hour would focus on developing partnerships between Michigan congregations and those in Mozambique. Pastor John Baku, a representative of several African churches, had been in Michigan for the past week. He had worked with Pastor Lane, Christian and Rosemary Gerber (Peg's mother) to explore ways of connecting church members from the two continents.

After welcoming everyone to the meeting, Pastor Becky offered a short prayer asking for God's blessing and guidance on their endeavor. Then she asked Ian to briefly summarize how this whole intercontinental affiliation began.

Ian thanked Becky and began telling his story. "Last January, Pastor John Baku and his congregation were our very own good Samaritans. When our research group from Michigan and Washington D.C. were stranded in a remote village…in a torrential downpour, we found we were unable to set up our camp or even cook outside. This good man, a stranger, a pastor, offered us refuge in his warm, dry church building. Then, with no hesitation he, his kind wife, and other generous church members shared their hot evening meals with us. For the next three days, they continued to provide shelter and food for all of us. They refused any form of payment, saying we were children of God…and it was their honor and Christian duty to help us in any way they could. We knew that we had received God's blessing through these wonderful people. In three short days, they had become our Christian brothers and sisters across the globe. Again, I thank you, Pastor John!"

There was clapping from those assembled, as well as appreciative nods.

Pastor John looked at Ian, then gestured to indicate all the people before him. "You and your church family, Professor, generously repaid our little church, ten-fold. Almost immediately, Interfaith Chapel sent us a sizable cash donation, along with a wide assortment of teaching and learning materials for our Sunday School. We also received boxes of children's picture books, markers, crayons, paper and other art supplies…things not readily available in our rural area. That was the beginning of an ongoing exchange between several people from both our communities. Thanks to the interpretation skills of Christian, here, and a couple of bilingual members of our church; letters were exchanged… between both adults and young people. Our members sent gifts of local art, crafts, hand-painted fabric and other things that you see displayed on the tables over there…to thank you for your generous donations. This meaningful relationship was quickly noticed by our bishop who wondered if other churches in his district might also become part of a partnership with Michigan congregations. He sent me here to see if some kind of official coordination agreement might be established."

"Since then," Christian added, "we have visited a number of area churches, explaining how other interested congregations might join us in our endeavor. After talking to local churches, Pastor John and I traveled to the Saginaw Valley area where, with the help of Mrs. Rosemary Gerber, we visited churches in her area…extending an invitation to be part of the project." Turning to Rosemary, Christian clasped his hands and bowed slightly, "Mrs. Gerber, because of your amazing networking skills and the community's high regard for you and your family, the impossible has become possible in a very short time. Two local churches have joined our effort and another is considering joining us, as well. Thank you for all you did to make this dream a real possibility for us all!"

Peg's mother looked at the faces around her and smiled sweetly. She began telling the group that although she lived in a small, rural community…its residents were globally aware, generous and had been eager to develop meaningful relationships with others in a faraway land. She said that she had brought representatives from two other congregations in addition to a member of her own church to be part of the meeting this night. All were ready to join churches in the Okemos area as they forged a bridge between Michigan Christians and those in Mozambique."

Pastor Rebecca thanked the Saginaw-area churches for joining them. She introduced and thanked members of two other Ingham County churches who were planning to participate, as well. She then asked the group to share questions and concerns before the official agreement was signed.

Several questions were raised: How big are the African congregations? How would they be able to communicate, due to the language differences? Were they all Protestant churches? Were women and children active participants in church programs? Were Peace Corps and other U.S. volunteer groups involved in these communities? What were the African people expecting or needing from their American partners? What benefits could the Michigan congregations expect to receive in return?

One of Chapel's members shared his own recent experiences. He described the substantive exchanges he'd been having with an African school teacher. He hoped that their exchanges were making both of them better educators. The exchanges had also begun to include students. Concluding, he said, "Yes, we may be able to help these churches with financial support and donations of supplies, but they can and will help us to better understand our world and give us an opportunity to demonstrate God's love through our gifts."

Satisfied that questions had been answered, representatives from the five other churches signed the partnership agreement that had already been signed by Pastor Lane and the African Bishop. After holding hands for a closing prayer and being thanked once again, the Saginaw visitors and other area church representatives were invited to stay for the remainder of the meeting or were excused to begin their drives home. Interfaith volunteers got up, stretched and spent a few minutes chatting with their new friends from Saginaw and the other local churches. As the visitors left, local chapel members refreshed their coffee and settled back for the next portion of the meeting.

Continuing with the agenda, Pastor Becky turned to Paul Franklin, who had just arrived, to report on the status of the newly-formed singles group called SCP or the "Singles Can Program." Paul explained that the group, less than six-months old, now boasted 22 active members. And, in addition to providing an opportunity for spiritual growth, new friendships and fun activities, the group had begun to reach out to home-bound members, as well as those in assisted living facilities in the area.

Several new Chapel members inquired about the ages and professions of SCP members.

"I'm not sure, probably 22 to 40, I'd say" was Paul's guess. "We have ethnic diversity and a fairly even number of men and women. Members' occupations seem to be quite diverse, as well. We've got an office manager, a welder, a firefighter, an attorney, a small business owner, an educator – that would be myself…and…hmmm, let's see…oh yeah… state government workers, a couple of health care providers and several others."

Another questioner wondered what was next on the group's agenda.

Paul turned to the questioner and nodded. "We do more than just pray and perform good works," he said. "In fact, after Thanksgiving we're planning a progressive dinner. Each course will feature foods from a different continent: Asia, South America, Europe and North America."

"Sounds great! Count me in," came a call from the back of the room.

The pastor thanked Paul for both his report and also this leadership. She mentioned that Paul had recently joined the church and had immediately become actively involved in the group.

The next report was on the high school youth group and

it was the Mahoneys turn to speak. Peg told the group that the high school youth group consists of 26 members this year. Instead of doing a Christmas-in-October workday as they did last year, the group voted to provide two days of assistance to an older couple who were charter members of Interfaith Chapel. The couple was trying to downsize before moving to a retirement facility. Since they had no family in Michigan, the youth group's help was invaluable to them.

Ian added, "The students spent all last Saturday responding to the directives and difficult decision-making of people parting with a lifetime of treasures. What to take, what to throw, what to donate…it can be overwhelming; but the kids were patient and hard-working. They sorted and organized household items for the move, packed those things the couple wanted to save for family members and set aside a sizable donation of goods for Refugee Services. Then they began preparing for a garage sale they plan to hold next Saturday for some of the furniture and other leftover items."

"The group," continued Peg, "has bi-weekly meetings where we discuss both religious and social issues of concern to the group. Recently, for instance, we had a heated debate prompted by a short video that was a spoof of how some young people believe the job market and future employers OWE them a job. We've also discussed recent mass shooting, racial and ethnic issues, safety in schools, politics and much more."

Pastor Becky praised the two leaders for bringing out the best in their young members. She noted what wonderful role models they both were. She also reported that some of the teens and their parents had requested meeting more often, perhaps every week.

Ian shook his head with a mixture of pride and personal disappointment. "While that's a great idea, I confess that Peg and I aren't really able to add two more monthly meetings to our calendars right now. We're spread about as thin as we can be at this time. We would, of course, be happy to welcome other adults who might be willing to share leadership responsibilities with us. We would love it, if others would step up and join our team. Believe me, it's well worth it!"

"Adding new blood with different experiences and creative ideas would only make our group stronger," Peggy went on. "I do hope that some of you or others you know might be willing to accept this invitation to serve our youth."

A new member to the congregation said she might be willing to assist and seemed eager to be part of a thriving group. Another new couple acknowledged that they had been involved with the high school group at their former church. Names and contact information were noted, and Peg and Ian promised to contact the willing volunteers soon.

In her closing benediction, the pastor rejoiced that although they were a small congregation without a church building or a large church staff, members had responded willingly to calls to serve the Lord. She thanked God that so many have stepped up to give their time, their resources, their prayers and their love to make this community and the world a better place for everyone. With that the meeting ended, and people began gathering their things.

Paul joined Ian and Peg as they prepared to leave. "Hey, guys, that was a great meeting. By the way, what are you doing Saturday night? Are you free to join me for dinner? I've been itching to cook Italian for someone besides myself… and, of course, the kids are welcome."

The couple exchanged looks and nodded, thinking what a treat that would be! Peg promised to bring Grandmother Gerber's fruit salad, since it would go with anything their host might choose to serve.

"Will six o'clock work for you?" Paul asked.

"Yes, thanks!" Ian replied. "We'll look forward to sharing your hospitality."

Peg added, "I think we'll ask Ida or Libby to spend that time with the children, so, if it works out…this time it will just be us grown-ups."

"Great! I'm looking forward to it, too," Paul agreed.

After picking up the twins, the Mahoneys drove home. The parents quietly reflected on what they had witnessed over the past hour-and-a-half while Mia and Mike chattered on about the games, activities and yummy snacks they'd had with Libby and the other kids. The Mahoneys were certainly involved with their family, their jobs, their community and their church. But as they thought ahead to the future…they both knew there was even more to come.

CHAPTER NINE

As the Mahoneys approached the home of Paul Franklin, Ian remarked, "You know, Peg, this will be our first dinner without the twins since we got back from our honeymoon. I love the little stinkers to pieces, but there are times when it's fun to have adult time alone with you — or with you and somebody like Paul."

"I know what you mean, so let's enjoy tonight for the special occasion that it is. "

Paul answered the door and ushered the Mahoneys into his living room.

"Welcome," said their host as he accepted a bowl from Peg. "I'm glad you could make it on such short notice…and thanks for the fruit salad, it looks delicious.

"Hey, Paul," Ian replied, "I have to admit, we were delighted to have a night out of the house. It's amazing how seldom that happens."

"I'm sure that's true with your busy schedules and TWO busy five-year-olds at home. Have a seat on the couch, what would you like to drink…I have both Coke and Sprite? Your choices?"

Peg and Ian sat down and looked around Paul's tastefully decorated – but totally male living room. Paul returned with the soft drinks and a tray of cheese and crackers. He placed them on the coffee table and took a seat opposite the Mahoneys. The threesome sat back and relaxed. They hadn't had a chance to chat the previous evening at school when the Mahoneys came for their parent-teacher conferences.

"So," Paul began, "how were the twins' conferences last night?"

Like all parents, Ian and Peg were eager to talk about how much they had enjoyed hearing about their children's progress. Peg answered Paul after glancing at Ian with a smile, "The kids are doing great…but the conferences, themselves, were…well, sort of like a sentimental journey for us."

"Why was that?" Paul looked confused. "Clue me in."

"Well," said Ian winking at his wife, "last year's conference was the first time Peg and I actually had a real conversation…that conversation eventually led us to the altar."

"I seem to be missing something here," Paul looked even more perplexed. After all, he thought he knew these two people. They seemed so practical and level-headed. "You talked about getting married at your first parent-teacher conference?"

Ian and Peggy broke out in merry laughter. Ian continued, "Well, not exactly. But it was at that conference that this lady conned me into spending the next Saturday morning at her church. She got me to help her and a group of teens complete a project they called Christmas in October." He looked fondly at his wife.

"Hold it, my dear," Peggy defended herself. "As I recall, you started it by saying you wanted to find a way to become active in some church programs. That's when I made the friendly suggestion that you could help us fix the front steps of an older couple at my church."

"Okay, okay…perhaps I did initiate the conversation," Ian laughed, "but the rest is history, Paul. We became co-advisors of the youth group and worked together with a great group of kids. It didn't take long for us to become friends. We were both avoiding commitments at the time, so it was far from anything romantic." He glanced at his wife and continued, "Of course, I couldn't help but notice that Miss Peggy was a very beautiful woman in addition to being the special caring teacher of my little ones."

Peggy blushed and slapped Ian playfully on the arm.

"Say, Paul," Ian teased turning to his host, "do any of your students have single mom's at home that you might snag?"

Peg opened her mouth in horror. "Ian!!!!" she exclaimed.

Laughing, Paul countered, "The nearest I come to it is a grandmother, a retired elementary principal, who accompanied the parents last night. She seemed to ask a million questions about our program. Hmmm…maybe she would be interested in another trip to the altar."

"Paul!" Peggy said with disgust. "You're as bad as my husband!"

Standing, Paul grabbed the empty cheese plate and said, "I guess that must be a compliment! Now, how about some real food? Come on into the kitchen, you guys."

Settling around the kitchen table, Paul proudly brought out his first course. It was an excellent interpretation of Pasta e Fagioli soup. It was followed with a light entree of linguini and shrimp, crusty Italian bread and Peg's fruit salad. Peg was impressed that her colleague really had learned to prepare authentic Italian cuisine. The meal was delicious!

As the school's administrator, Paul was very interested in how students in his school were progressing – especially Ian and Peg's two kindergartners.

Ian explained that he had spent a wonderful couple of hours observing in their classroom prior to conferences, so that he was prepared to ask reasonable questions. He reported that their teacher had said both Mike and Mia were doing nicely.

"He's being too modest," said their proud new mother. "Both have very long attention spans for five-year-olds. They both like to color, especially when it comes to making creative maps of the world. We talk a lot about Ian's work in Africa; and we just got back from our European honeymoon, so that might be why they're so interested in world geography."

Mia, as the family's reader, had taken great strides in learning to do cursive writing — something still taught in Montessori kindergartens. Mike was interested in math and problem solving. He apparently also liked to work with the bells. They wondered if there was some relationship between math and music.

"I don't know about scientific research on the topic," responded Paul, "but I have several relatives who seem to have that connection, also. One of my uncles is a high school math teacher and also plays the cello in the community orchestra. I also have a cousin who is an actuary for an insurance company – and she's an accomplished pianist."

"Hmmm…" mused Peg. "Maybe I should consider playing some classic music in the background while my students tackle math activities."

Peg and Ian helped Paul clear the table, then their host brought out some spumoni ice cream for dessert along with both tea and coffee. Ian was glad that they hadn't made the mistake of bringing a bottle of wine, something they had considered doing. Apparently, Paul wasn't much of a drinker, either.

"Hey, Paul, tell us about this creative sports program that you've been hinting about," Peggy suggested.

After swallowing a big spoonful of ice cream, Paul said, "Well, so far, it's only in embryonic form, but I've had the go-ahead from the Board to explore the possibility, and Grace is all for it."

"Please tell us more," Ian prompted. "A creative sports program? What's that all about?"

Paul admitted that he'd always been interested in youth sports. After joining the staff, he noticed that the school's gym seemed to be under-utilized. He began to think about how to use the gym to fill what appeared to be missing at the school – organized sports. He thought it might be a good idea to start a basketball league for boys and girls. One of the parents had told him that there used to be several opportunities for youngsters to play informal sports. One was a church softball league and the other was a parent-managed program that involved soft ball, flag football, soccer, as well as basketball. But in recent years, there hadn't been a sports program of any kind at the school.

"I remember informal sports programs when I was a kid, but by the time I was old enough to participate, we'd moved to the state of Washington," commented Ian.

"We never had such programs where I lived," admitted Peg. "Rural kids had too much farm work and too many life-skill-type 4-H projects expected of them to spend time in organized sports outside of school." Then she added, "Besides, I know that some elementary educators question having any form of competition for youngsters. It's too bad for those kids who have true athletic talent. They're the ones who probably benefit most from the programs you've described."

Paul shook his head, "Not really, Peg. All children benefit from working on teams and perfecting their large motor skills. But it's not just physical development, there are many other skills that are enhanced by playing sports. Things like planning strategies, thinking about what one's opponents might do and adjusting to it, handling victory and defeat, supporting teammates and many more. There are so many benefits to sports, that I could go on all night. Just take it from me…participating in sports provides kids with many learning opportunities not available elsewhere."

"Yes," agreed Peg, "I guess I hadn't thought about it that way."

The Mahoneys told Paul they thought his idea sounded promising, but they also said it sounded like a lot of work — not only planning the program but also getting partner-schools, promoting the program and recruiting both participants and the volunteers needed to make it work.

"Yes, I know," Paul sighed. "I've been doing a lot of online research, getting to know the pros and cons of all sorts of elementary competitive programs and trying to generate a list of possible partners."

He'd discovered that there were quite a few private K-8 schools in the area. Many of them were Catholic or had other religious affiliations — Lutheran and Baptist and maybe even one non-denominational. He thought some of them might be interested in participating in a program such as the one he was envisioning.

"Don't forget there are other private Montessori or Montessori-like schools in East Lansing and Okemos as well as several public and/or charter Montessori programs in the county. They might see this as a way for the Montessorians to band together," Peg suggested.

"Another group I've been wondering about is the home-school crowd," Paul offered. "I know they foster socialization opportunities. In some states they band together to hire a licensed teacher to instruct the older students in algebra, physics, chemistry and other demanding subjects. I know they also have home-school music programs and even sports leagues for older kids…I'm just not sure what's available for them in our community yet. If they're not already participating, perhaps they would also like to join something like I'm proposing?"

Peg said that she thought she remembered that home-school numbers are not exact, because Michigan is one of a minority of states that doesn't require home-school families to report to the state. Likewise, private school enrollment is also voluntarily reported.

Paul nodded, "Yes, I was surprised I couldn't just pull up numbers of local home-schoolers and the name of an organizer of some kind. Some data I located stated that about 3% of school-aged children are home-schooled in the U.S. If Michigan families follow national trends that would equate to about 50,000 home-schoolers in the state. But how many home-schooled children does Michigan or Ingham County actually have? And what are their ages? I'm afraid at this point it's really anyone's guess! I suppose the place to start is with the private schools, while I keep digging on the home-school possibility."

"Sounds as if you've got your spare-time work cut out for you!" Ian said. "Would MSU folks be interested and willing to assist in anyway?"

"I'm not sure," Paul replied, "but I intend to pursue all possible avenues in the next month or two. This program would be a far cry from those high-pressure, costly programs for middle schoolers run by for-profit outfits. There are plenty of statewide and even interstate competitive programs out there already. I'm definitely thinking local…and affordable…and instructional…and fun for both participants and facilitators."

Peg knew something about the history of Ojibwa Montessori School. Institutional memory was a handy resource to have. In the early years, MSU wasn't even willing to come and visit the Montessori classrooms. The education department on campus focused on public, not private schools, and certainly not "out of the norm" educational programming. However, many public school teachers did come to visit Ojibwa after hearing about the program. Many professors also admitted that Montessori education was a hot topic at professional meetings. As time went on, it gradually became accepted as the exceptionally-effective program it was. Fortunately, by the time Peggy Gerber was a college student, Michigan State was more than willing for her and others to accept part-time employment at the school. Now, of course, Montessori programs even exist in public schools. Fortunately for Ojibwa and the children lucky enough to attend, times have changed and now Montessori principles are widely respected and emulated.

"Paul, I think several public school systems offer organized sports for kids through their community education programs," Peg offered. "I recently saw a flier describing such a program in East Lansing. It's designed for kindergarten and first graders, and if I remember properly, I think it focuses on skill development in dribbling, passing and shooting the ball."

"Really, that's a new one for me. Do you remember what it's called, Peg?" Paul asked.

"I think it was something like Buddy Basketball," she said.

"I'll certainly check it out," Paul said, "and see what I can learn about it. I wonder if it's only for public school kids."

"Good luck, my friend," Ian said standing and patting Paul on the back. "Risk-taking is never easy whether it's trying to start a new program for kids or unlocking the mysteries of plant science. Go for it, I'd say! Let us know if we can help in any way. I know our kids will be the first on the list, if your idea becomes a reality, right honey?"

"You bet!" Peg added enthusiastically.

As Ian headed for the door, he said to his new friend, "Many thanks for the gourmet dinner, Paul, and a chance for some interesting thought-provoking adult conversation!"

"You are most welcome," Paul responded. "Getting to know the two of you better means a lot to me. By the way, who's watching the twins tonight? I was going to ask earlier, then I forgot."

"Our lifesaver, Ida, is with the kids," Peg answered.

Peg explained that Ida, the family's part-time housekeeper and former nanny hadn't been able to spend much time with the twins lately. She had offered to help them create their Halloween costumes – and tonight had been a good time to start the process. Michael wanted to be a professor this year, and Mia was determined to be a Tai Chi instructor. Mrs. H, as the children called her, was designing and constructing the costumes so that the kids could use them after trick-or-treating. The professor's commencement gown would serve as a bathrobe and the Tai Chi outfit, a pair of PJ's.

"Practical use of resources, I'd say," Paul said. "You are fortunate to have that kind of help."

"We call it a blessing!" Peg said adamantly.

After another round of thank-yous and good byes, the Mahoneys headed for home. Once in the car, they talked about how delightful it was to have spent such a pleasant evening with their new friend, and how strange it felt to spend an evening without the kids. They both admitted, though, that they looked forward to kissing those little, tousled, dream-filled heads as soon as they got home.

CHAPTER TEN

With trick-or-treat behind them, the twins were ready to think about Thanksgiving. This year, they were again planning, with Mommy's help, to bake and decorate a tray of cut-out turkeys to take to the celebration at the Lanes next door. Ian insisted on Pastor Becky accepting a check to cover the cost of the turkey, as well – just as he had the year before.

Ida volunteered to make mashed potatoes and gravy and at least two kinds of dressing – and to manage the basic kitchen duties. Peg's friend, Jodie, agreed to contribute the green bean casserole and sweet potatoes topped with toasty marshmallows. Another young couple who had moved from Boston the year before, Randy and Heather Martin, promised to bring their special cranberry, apple and walnut salad.

Rod Lane also extended an invitation to the retired librarian, Martha Webb, who had helped him edit his soon-to-be-released book on Chief Okemos. He'd encouraged her to invite a friend or relative, as well. Becky, also suggested including Ian's colleague from Africa, Christian Rosario, as well as Peg's friend, Paul Franklin. Chris gratefully accepted and offered to bring some special cashews from Mozambique. Paul, who had been wondering how he would spend the day, appreciated the invitation and said he would bake several loaves of fresh bread.

Martha Webb was pleased to be asked to join the Lanes

for Thanksgiving, since her family was overseas this year. Shortly before the big day, she caught her neighbor when both were outside picking up their mail. "Hi, Jordan, I can't believe how long it's been since we've chatted…and we only live a few steps apart! Hey, My Dear, I've been meaning to call and ask if you have plans for Thanksgiving."

"Not yet," Jordan said, smiling. "I'm sorry I haven't popped over…I've just been so busy at work. It's funny, Martha, I recently joined the University Club and was actually planning to invite you for Thanksgiving dinner there. Would you like to join me?"

Martha laughed, "Aren't we the busy ones! That would have been a lovely treat, I'm sure, Dear, but recently I accepted a dinner invitation from Rod Lane. He's a high school history teacher, and I've been assisting him with his book on Chief Okemos. He's a wonderful storyteller but needed help in editing the manuscript before it went to the publisher."

"So, you stepped in to help. Why am I not surprised?" Jordan said appreciatively. "As a former librarian and avid reader, you're the perfect editor for him."

"Of course, I refused payment…so he insisted on including me for Thanksgiving dinner, a celebration that he and his wife have hosted for many years. Plus, he encouraged me to bring along a relative or special friend. I accepted immediately and knew just whom to invite to accompany me. He mentioned that some of their neighbors and an assortment of others, new or relatively new in the community, were also invited." She touched Jordan gently on the arm, "I do hope that you'll accept, Dear!"

Why not? Jordan thought.

"Do we need to contribute anything to the meal?" she asked.

"I asked Rod that same question," Martha replied, "but he

assured me that more food was definitely not needed, since others were filling in the gaps. So, I suggested that we bring a centerpiece for the table. He agreed, so that's an easy assignment for us."

Jordan offered to order something appropriate from the florist. She mentioned that she needed the Lane's address, so the arrangement could be delivered the day before Thanksgiving. Martha promised to give her a call right away.

When she called to give Jordan the address, she told her that she thought the Lane home might be in the same neighborhood as Jordan's professor friend and his family. She said she hoped they would be on the guest list, also, because it would be nice for Jordan to have a couple of other familiar faces at the table.

Preparations for the Thanksgiving feast went forward, and the day FINALLY arrived, according to the twins. The sun shone brightly, and the clear blue sky made everyone happy after a week of gray clouds. A smiling Rod Lane welcomed guests as they arrived, and he invited them to gather around the fireplace where a warm fire blazed. As people got acquainted, he passed around steaming mugs of spiced cider and indicated the bowls of extra-large seasoned cashews that Christian had brought.

The dining table looked lovely with its fall arrangement of mums in a beautifully-woven cornucopia basket. The glassware glistened on the snowy tablecloth while the holiday napkins added festive color to the table setting.

Jordan and Martha were greeted warmly by their hostess, who said simply, "Please call me Becky, that's what most folks do. You, I believe," she said turning to Jordan, "already know our next-door neighbors, the Mahoneys. This young man," she said pointing to Christian, "is Christian Rosario, Ian's hard-working graduate assistant."

After exchanging pleasantries with Chris, Jordan and Martha turned to find Peg approaching. She grabbed Martha's hand and said how delighted she was to finally meet the famous Martha. Then she swept the pair into the kitchen to meet Ida Harding. Martha saw an apron, donned it and immediately started helping Ida mash potatoes. Peg took Jordan's arm and pulled her over to meet her friends, Jodie and Ben.

"This, is Jodie Allen, my college roommate and long-time best friend. She's a physician's assistant. Ben is really Dr. Ben Allen, a surgeon who works with physically-challenged children. And this is B.J., their son. He's a student in our Montessori preschool," Peg said, adding, "and this is Dr. Jordan Taylor. She works with Ian on campus."

Jordan was immediately interested in the work Dr. Ben was doing and hoped she'd be able to ask him about it before the day was over. She was glad she had come. She noticed a young man over by the fireplace. He looked a lot like Rod, so Jordan figured he must be the Lane's college-aged son.

After meeting the Martins and their baby daughter, Jordan joined the larger group as they all found seats around the table. The Mahoney twins wanted to sit by B.J., so they quickly grabbed two empty chairs, and their parents settled beside them.

Mia piped up unexpectedly, "Can I say the prayer today, Pastor Becky?"

Surprised, everyone turned to Mia. "Why, that would be wonderful. Everyone, let's join hands while our Mia gives thanks."

As everyone reached out to create a chain of friendship around the table, Mia straightened, cleared her throat and closed her eyes. "Because it's Thanksgiving, God" she began earnestly, "I want to thank you for the very best gift of all...

our new mommy! And...I want to thank you for all these new friends...and for the turkey! Amen."

Tears sprang to the eyes of several of those around the table as they mumbled their own "Amens"...and Peg leaned down to hug her new daughter.

"Well," said Pastor Becky, "I have to say...that's the best Thanksgiving prayer I've ever heard...and I've heard a lot of them! Sit down everyone...let's eat!"

"If I did believe in prayer," thought Jordan, surprising herself, "I'd have to say, that's a prayer any God would hear."

Everyone sat down and reached for a napkin. Much to Jordan's surprise, she spotted Peg's Montessori colleague at the other end of the long table.

"Paul Franklin!" she thought, realizing his name was hard to forget. "Oh, no! Not him again! Oh well, thank goodness he's at the far end of the table, I should have no trouble keeping my distance from him."

Chattering had begun around the table when Pastor Becky clinked her water glass to get everyone's attention. "Friends," she began, "thank you all for coming. It's such a joy to have all of you in our home on this special day. We have a special Lane Thanksgiving tradition...and we would like you to be a part of it today. If you are willing, we would like each of you to share something for which you are grateful this year...or describe a special Thanksgiving memory from the past. I think we would all agree...our Mia started us off nicely...thank you, Mia!"

The guests looked at one another for a moment, then Randy Martin from Massachusetts spoke up and said he and Heather were thankful for the safe arrival of their new baby daughter, Allison.

The Allens then told about a particularly difficult surgery that had saved a toddler's life recently. Dr. Ben had been the surgeon and Jodie had assisted.

Michael said, "Well, you already know God gave us a new mommy this year, but I'm also glad our friend, B.J. moved here!"

"Me, too!" quipped B.J.

Ian looked at Peg and said, "How could I not add my thanks to The One who led this special woman to us…someone who loved us enough to say 'yes' and become a Mahoney!" Peg blushed, smiled at her husband, and squeezed his hand under the table.

Peg simply gestured toward her husband and two new children, "What can I say…I think you all know what I'm thankful for this year."

Libby expressed her appreciation for having been able to participate in the week-long trip to an Indian Reservation in South Dakota last spring. Her brother, Bob, was grateful he was able to take several online courses, thereby allowing him to graduate early and start his Peace Corps orientation sooner than expected. He said he was now praying his assignment would be in Africa.

Christian's comments surprised Ian but not Pastor Becky. He said he was grateful to have had time to reflect on his career choices and for the extended conversations he'd had with Pastor John from Mozambique.

Becky indicated her joy in the chapel's growing membership and the success of several of its new programs. She mentioned that she had great hopes for the newest initiative, "Singles Can."

"Wow," thought Jordan, "that woman really had me fooled. I never would have guessed she was a preacher. She seems so normal."

The pastor's comments prompted Paul to speak up. "I have to say that I feel that it was something more than blind luck that led me to my new life in Michigan. Starting a challenging new job, making great friends and joining a wonderful church…all make me feel most blessed this Thanksgiving."

Ida offered thanks for her new granddaughter, opportunities to contribute to the community and the good news that this very spring her dream of going to England would finally come true.

That left only Rod and the two female guests who had been silent so far.

Jordan looked around the group, hesitated and then in a soft voice — almost a whisper — cleared her throat and began. "This fall I unexpectedly discovered something that has been missing in my life. Something I've longed for since childhood…a caring adult who accepts me unconditionally…flaws and all. I finally have my very own 'grandmother'…this dear lady, my wonderful new friend, Martha Webb."

Peg felt a tear spring to the corner of her eye unexpectedly…as she and everyone else nodded in support of Jordan.

Before Martha could respond, Rod spoke up, "Jordan, I move to second your motion that Martha Webb is one special friend. She's not old enough to be my grandmother, but she came to my rescue, as well. Martha's a miracle worker. She generously shared her expertise and agreed to edit my book about Chief Okemos. Without her smarts, I'd still be looking for a publisher. Martha, please accept my heartfelt thanks for your contribution to the soon-to-be-released book." Clapping and cheers of wonderment greeted this news, since several guests were not even aware that Rod was an author! Others were delighted to hear that they would soon be reading his long-awaited book.

Martha was quite overcome by these unexpected accolades. Looking around the table, she smiled sweetly at those assembled. As the oldest one present, it seemed appropriate that she would provide a finale to the Thanksgiving tributes.

"All of us," she began, "have recognized the richness of the lives we enjoy in this community. With God's help, we can continue to make a difference in this world by generously sharing the many gifts we are blessed to have. I never dreamed when my son went overseas and rented his home to this young woman, Jordan Taylor, that she would become the granddaughter I never had. I'm so very pleased to have her in my life!"

Pastor Becky cleared her throat and said, "I want to thank each one of you for sharing such meaningful thoughts today. I think all of us are blessed to have learned something special about each of our friends around this table. Now...does anyone want seconds on turkey?"

Friendly chatter continued as guests passed around the potatoes and casseroles again...refilling their plates. People pleaded that they had no room for dessert, but when Becky brought out her fresh pumpkin, pecan, and apple pies and a tray of beautifully-decorated turkey cookies...no one could refuse. After the last morsel had been licked off forks, people began to pull themselves up from the table.

As Bob rose, he invited everyone to join him around the fireplace for a traditional group sing. With the accompaniment of his guitar, the group's voices joined in a robust chorus of "We Gather Together," "Over the River and Through the Woods" and other popular Thanksgiving melodies. In a salute to the upcoming winter season, they closed by singing a rousing "Jingle Bells."

Paul turned and found himself just behind Jordan. He took the occasion to speak briefly. "Nice to see you again," he said with a smile.

"Likewise," was her brief reply as she started to turn

quickly away.

"Hey, Jordan, you heard Becky mention the 'Singles Can' program at the chapel?" Paul continued. "I've actually attended some of their activities. It's really a most interesting group of people…sort of religious, but not preachy. We're having a progressive dinner next Saturday. I'd be happy to have you attend as my guest."

"Uh, thank you…but I'm afraid I'm…tied up with some graduate students on Saturday," Jordan dismissed him rather rudely as she hurried off to find her coat and see if Martha was ready to leave.

"So much for trying," thought the Montessori Director. Paul mentally decided he had better forget about THAT one. She was obviously not interested in pursuing any kind of – even a friendly – relationship with him.

And so ended the day.

CHAPTER ELEVEN

Peg sighed after the last of her students departed for home. This year was taking longer than usual to normalize, perhaps because, so far no class leaders, such as Mike and Mia, had emerged. "I'll go to the library and check on that set of primary books that just arrived," she thought, "By the time I'm finished reviewing them, I'll be able to pick the kids up from their Tai Chi class."

She entered the school library with an armful of books and settled into an inviting rocking chair to begin reviewing the books. Just then, Paul came into the room.

A friendly, "Hi there, Mrs. Mahoney," was how he announced his arrival. "I'll bet you still look around to see who's being addressed when you hear that name."

"Yes," smiled his friend, "I was Peggy Gerber for a long time. When I hear 'Mrs. Mahoney' I still look around, but my mother-in-law is nowhere to be found. I must confess, though, it does have a nice ring to it. Don't you think?"

Paul nodded and then asked, "Can you spare a minute for me to update you on the basketball project?"

"Of course, Paul, I am really only killing time until the Tai Chi class ends," Peg responded, setting aside the book she had just opened. "I do enjoy watching Dr. Wang and the children, but I don't want to observe them too often. The kids need to feel like they can be on their own. So, have a seat, Paul, and tell me the good news."

Paul sat down at a nearby library table. "Thanks for giving me the contact list for both the public and private Montessori schools in the area. I'm sending them a letter next week outlining the basketball project and requesting a time to meet to discuss it."

"Good! How about the Catholic and other religious schools?" Peggy asked. "Have you made any headway with them?"

Paul shook his head, "I can't believe there are still so many Catholic elementary schools operating. I don't think that's true in my part of Virginia. I was also surprised by the number of protestant schools."

"To tell you the truth, I've never given them much thought," Peg admitted. "Guess I've always been too busy worrying about our school enrollment remaining stable or…increasing."

"I think I now have a complete list of all the private and religious schools that offer K-8 programs, and their principals," Paul said. "I'm still collecting data on numbers of students by grade and gender."

"Have you decided which grades you want to include in your program?" she asked.

Paul leaned forward and rested his elbows on his knees, "For the first year, I'm thinking we should include K-3 students. Perhaps a K-1 and 2-3 team, since there are some third-grade boys who are quite tall and hefty. If we put all the kids together, those big kids would have a huge developmental advantage, and it could even be dangerous for the younger kids. Obviously, we want all the kids to have equal playing time, so smaller teams would allow each child to play more."

"Will you have both boys and girls on the same team…

it sounds like it, if you're only having one team for K-1 and 2-3," Peg wondered out loud. "I know many of the girls also like to play and compete."

"Well, first of all…it depends on how many kids sign up! Hopefully, there will be enough kids that we'll have a choice about that. But, if we do have enough boys and girls to have separate teams, then we will have to address that question… and it's a challenging question to resolve," Paul admitted he'd been thinking about it. "I honestly don't know what's best. All I know is both genders deserve an opportunity to develop the skills necessary to play the sport…and I'm leaning toward combined teams at K-1 and perhaps separate teams at 2-3. I really have to get help from the experts on this one. Surely there's research on the subject. So far, I just haven't found it. I did make an appointment with someone in the recreation department on campus to discuss the gender question. Actually, I have a whole list of topics to discuss."

"Leave it to you to spend time contacting those in-the-know. I have to give you an 'A' for effort and creativity, so far!" His teacher friend was clearly impressed. "You haven't mentioned the home-schoolers? Have you had any luck finding out about them?"

Paul shook his head. "Funny you should ask…I'm finding that's going to be the most nut to crack. However, I've recruited a helper who may have an inside track in identifying a few local home-school parents. Apparently, there are groups of those parents who meet regularly to share their experiences. Of course, there are also the publishing companies who supply instructional materials for home-school use. They might be willing to share names and addresses of their clients or even forward information to those clients on my behalf. It seems like they would want to provide positive opportunities for the children they serve. Anyway, it won't hurt to ask."

"Where did you unearth this new helper?" Peg was intrigued. "Who is it? Anybody I know?"

"I doubt it," he said. "Her name is Tammy Sue Randolph, and she's the woman I contacted regarding that special basketball skills program that's offered in East Lansing. You remember, the one that teaches basketball skills to kindergarten and first graders...skills like dribbling, passing and shooting the ball."

"You mean Buddy Basketball?" she prompted.

"Yeah," he nodded, "that's the one you read about in that Continuing Education flier. She was very helpful when I contacted her, per your suggestion. She followed up by sending me all the materials I asked about. I got their application form, parent consent materials, medical approval form...even the security background check procedures they use. It has been most helpful...thanks to your tip!"

Laughing, Peg said, "Well, if all I have to do is give a tip to get all that credit...I should give tips more often! It sounds like Mrs. Randolph turned out to be a great resource!"

"Well, actually," Paul corrected, "it's MS...and you're not going to believe the coincidence! Remember when I mentioned the progressive dinner that the Singles Can group was having the Saturday after Thanksgiving?"

"Of course. We were sorry that Jordan wasn't able to go with you."

Paul shrugged, "Well...she obviously wasn't that interested in spending time with me or even becoming my friend. I was just reaching out to help her meet some more people. Whatever...."

"I guess you might call it prying, but I was wondering why she said 'no?' Did she even give you a reason?" she asked her friend.

"She told me she had a conflict...some kind of activity with the graduate students in her department," Paul replied.

"Oh, yeah," Peg offered, "I think Ian mentioned that she told him a group of grad students were going to a landscaping show at Meijer Gardens in Grand Rapids that day. It's too bad she couldn't get back in time for the dinner." Peg secretly wondered how hard Jordan tried to make it work.

"Oh, well, I guess even this dumb athlete knows when to move on!" Paul said a little embarrassed. "What I was about to say is that, much to my surprise, Tammy Sue was at the progressive dinner. She's apparently been a member of the 'Singles Can' group for some time but wasn't at our recent meetings because she was busy helping her sister. That's why I hadn't met her."

"Then she's local...with family here?" Peg wanted to know.

Paul went on to explain that Tammy Sue's family had only been in town for a year or two. He said that her sister's husband came here to join a local family law firm, and that the sister had started her own company as an event planner after she arrived. Tammy Sue came to Michigan about 18 months ago to work in her sister's business but got a job with East Lansing Community Education soon after. She coordinates several of the leisure and recreational programs that they offer and has really enjoyed the challenge.

"Where did the family come from? The name Tammy Sue sounds southern to me," Peg suggested.

"Yaes, m'aam," Paul answered with an exaggerated drawl. "That she is...a real 'Georgia Peach.' She's blond, not very tall and has a noticeable southern accent."

"Men!" Peg said disgustedly. "She sounds like a real go-getter in spite of your chauvinistic remark. I'll look forward to meeting her. How's she planning to identify the home-schoolers?"

"Her office collects all sorts of data about school-aged children," Paul explained. "As you said, Michigan is one of about a dozen states that doesn't require home-school registration figures. They do have general contact information, though, if parents are involved in formal or even informal home-school parent organizations. That seems to be about the best way to proceed."

"So, how long do you think it'll take her to gather that information? It sounds as if she's plenty busy already," Peg said.

The man's face reddened. "I…well…she said she'd have it by this Saturday. It won't actually be that hard, because they have a lot of the info already. Because home-schoolers are part of the community…they can join community education programs, which are open to anyone living in East Lansing. Anyway, she invited me over for brunch to pick it up. Since gourmet cooking is one of her hobbies, it should be an interesting and delicious morning."

"Was she one of the cooks at the progressive dinner?" Peg continued to pry. "Wasn't it an international theme? So, what else did you end up having?"

"Tammy Sue's group provided the desserts…French pastries from Europe. They were fabulous! The Asian group chose Japanese appetizers. I was in the North American group, and we contributed a big spinach salad and homemade yeast rolls. The main course was a beef dish from Brazil in South America. What a feast!" Paul said patting his stomach.

"Sounds like it was a very special evening, Paul," Peg said sincerely. "I'm so glad you've become part of the singles group at church and have had a chance to make some new friends. That can be hard without a group, like Singles Can."

"Pastor Becky certainly had the right idea when she proposed this particular group to your congregation," Paul agreed.

"MS Randolph seems to have many talents…and endless energy," Peg suggested. "She sounds like she'd be fun to hang out with. Where'd she go to school?"

"Her degree's in marketing, and she got it at Emery University in Atlanta," he responded.

Peg thought for a moment. "Atlanta. Hmmm, did she by any chance work for Coca Cola?"

"You are right on the money," Paul said, surprised that she knew about Coke's headquarters.

"She was in their brand management division for a few years. Hmmm…do you think those skills might come in handy when marketing a kid basketball league?"

"Shame on you for harvesting her considerable talent for your own devices!" Peg said playfully. "Now that you've met someone you like, there are lots of holiday events coming up. Do you know about the annual Silver Bells Parade in downtown Lansing? It includes the Christmas tree lighting at the State Capitol. In fact, I think it's this weekend."

Paul followed with, "What about Christmas musical events? I imagine that high schools, churches as well as campus groups have lots of holiday performances. I've always looked forward to performances of the 'Messiah.'"

Peg responded, "Yeah, me, too…and many choirs encourage willing members of the audience to join them for the final chorus. Of course, most churches hold Christmas Eve services. Interfaith Chapel held it's service in a little church in the Meridian Township Historical Park last year. I wasn't able to go, 'cause I was at home with my family. We'll all be at the farm again this year. How about you? What are your plans for Christmas?"

"My sister, her husband and I plan to fly to Florida to check on Dad and Uncle Bud. They seem to both be doing well, but because it was Christmas when we lost Mom, it's important to be together to celebrate her life as well as the birth of the Christ child."

Peg looked at her watch. "Oh, my…look at the time. I have to get to the gym to pick up the kids from Tai Chi. I'm already a couple of minutes late!"

They both got up and headed for the door. On the way out, Paul said, "Many thanks for helping this newcomer in so many ways, Peg. I always find our conversations so enlightening. Who says that a single man and a happily married woman can't develop a solid friendship? At least that's how I see it."

"I certainly agree, Paul. For me…it's almost like having a fourth brother!" She laughed, then got serious. "I do hope you find the other kind of female friendship, though, Paul… the kind that leads to happiness and lifelong commitment. I want that for you…both Ian and I do."

"Well, I guess we'll see. The thing I know about meaningful relationships is that it takes time to learn about one another…time to share experiences…time to grow together. The good news is…I've got all the time there is." Paul waved as he turned into his office.

"Interesting conversation," thought Peg as she headed to the gym to pick up the kids. "I'm glad that this very nice man was not hurt by Jordan Taylor's brush off. He seems to have taken it in stride…and he's doing the right thing to continue spending time with interesting new female friends. I guess it's best to leave the matchmaking to God."

CHAPTER TWELVE

In the days following Thanksgiving, Peg noticed a big change in her husband. He seemed detached. He'd been spending more evenings at his campus office; and when he was home, he was at his desk late into the night poring over his computer. He'd even been a little short with the twins, something she'd never noticed before. She knew he was concerned about his grant project, but he hadn't shared what those concerns were. Peg had done her best to become familiar with Mozambique and read as much as she could find about Jatropha. Lately, she'd also tried to keep the children occupied in the evenings so they would not interrupt their dad's nightly reads.

After his meeting with the funders of both the Department of Energy project and the USAID-supported training program, she finally approached him and asked how the three days at the English Inn had gone.

"Oh, Peg, I'm so sorry. I've been waiting for the right time to explain my recent obsession with work," replied a very exhausted-looking professor. "The meetings went well. They were challenging, but very productive…much as I'd expected."

"So, your long hours at home and at the office were in preparation for those three days?" Peg asked.

His response surprised her. He explained that recently,

he'd become aware of some major political shifts in Mozambique. At the same time, there'd been a number of remarkable advances in the use of Jatropha seeds to produce biodiesel. Things were happening so quickly on so many fronts that Ian was beginning to wonder if he was in over his head.

"Are you saying that others may be eclipsing your work with Jatropha?" she asked, concerned.

"Not exactly," he acknowledged. "As long as I'm working in the lab on plant genetics…improving plant hardiness and increasing seed production…I'm okay. At times I may become frustrated and disappointed, but as long as I'm focused on the science and accomplishing my goal, I know what I'm doing. It's all the extraneous factors…like politics and agricultural decisions being made halfway around the world… that concern me. Things I have no way to control."

"Well, those are certainly concerning, but like you said, they're things about which you have no control. I just know that with all the success you've been having with your genetic trials, the real Jatropha breakthrough will happen in your laboratory, Dear!" was her supportive assessment. She just felt so powerless in her ability to help him with this frustrating situation.

Ian turned to her and grabbed her hand. He looked deeply into her eyes and said sincerely, "Peggy, without you holding things together here at home and spending so much time with Mike and Mia…I just don't know what I would do!"

The question that crossed her mind as she listened to his concerns was what — if anything — had actually changed with the Department of Energy project? Previously, it had seemed fairly simple. Hopefully, the Mozambique internal conflicts would not result in a reduction of funding for Ian's project. That would be disastrous.

Ian explained that the energy department funders were delighted with the progress he and his team had made in isolating the genes and modifying them. The trials were showing excellent outcomes. The work that David Mason and Ian were doing had actually resulted in better results than expected. Dave's experience as a regular plant breeder before returning to get the advanced degree brought a unique perspective and had been extremely beneficial to his work on this project.

Moreover, the training program for Mozambique farmers that Kevin and Jay would be leading was getting high marks from the USAID's supervisory team. Another grad student, Dana Allen, was planning to accompany them, as well. She had worked in Washington for her local congressman who chaired an important agriculture subcommittee. In fact, USAID was so impressed, they were thinking about pledging additional funds. Their enthusiastic support had caught the attention of many officials at MSU.

That being said, Ian told Peggy that it had been decided to put a hold on Ian's trip to Mozambique planned for early next year. That likely meant no trip home for Christian, either. It was thought that their time would be better spent in the lab, continuing their work on improving the quality and quantity of the Jatropha oil seeds...especially considering their recent progress with the trials.

"I'm also thinking I need to begin pursuing contacts in Japan and India, where researchers are also focusing on the quantity of seeds produced," Ian went on.

Peg responded, "I can see how developing relationships with researchers there could possibly lead to quicker results. But I imagine, everyone wants to be the first to discover genetic breakthroughs...there's plenty of monetary incentive to do so." Peg immediately grasped both the benefits and challenges of pursuing such a partnership. "I wonder if Japanese and Indian researchers would be willing to work with you. And would that mean no more trips to Mozambique?"

"I'm not sure, Peg," Ian responded. "At this point, it's hard to say. There's now a U.S. agricultural attaché assigned to Mozambique. The plan is for Dana…with her Washington experience and her interest in political action…to accompany the attaché to meetings with government officials while she's there."

Ian went on to remind Peg about another project he'd learned about after his return from Mozambique. It was a pilot project in another part of the country. The local government in that region had actually financed the construction of a small processing plant. By using plant seeds from nearby farms, they were successfully making biodiesel to supply their local needs. Perhaps that model might appeal to the national officials and lead them to fund other small operations.

"In the short run," he said, "several smaller operations might make more sense than beginning with a huge export goal. I know that originally, the foreign investors wanted to create a commodity great enough to export. And, of course, I believe they can…but I also think it takes time to build the infrastructure necessary for such a plan to succeed. Dana and the attaché will be floating that possibility, as well."

Maybe it was the pragmatic Michigan farmer in Peg… but she had to agree that starting small is probably a better choice than going all-in before the system is able to handle it. It was comforting to know that, once again, the two of them agreed — probably because deep-down, they both were very practical people.

Now that he had opened the dam that had been holding back all of his ideas about Mozambique, he wanted to share them – all of them – with Peg.

"Another thing we talked about when we were over there..." Ian continued, "was the idea of establishing contract farming...either with individual farmers or groups of farmers. Do you know what I'm talking about?"

Peg nodded and said, "Well, not how it works in Mozambique, but I know a lot of the sugar beet growers in our county sign contracts with processors to provide a certain tonnage of beets each fall. That assures the processors of having ample beets to meet their demand; and, at the same time, it frees the growers from having to worry about finding markets for their beets when they're ready to harvest."

"That's pretty much how it works in any country," Ian said, once again impressed by his wife's understanding of the complexities of agriculture. "I believe Dana's dad belongs to a farm co-op that contracts with the local elevator for soy beans. She's very familiar with the process, which may not be the case for the attaché, so it'll be good to have her in the discussion. I had some doubts about what Dana would be able to contribute to my project, but now I'm really glad that I took a chance on her. Her contributions, though quite different from the other two grad students, have been quite significant."

"Will contract farming be part of the training program that the MSU team delivers?" Peg wanted to know.

"I hope so," he answered. "Eight-ten years ago, a similar project was tried, but it failed miserably. I truly believe that the earlier attempt failed because the investors got ahead of themselves. They jumped in prematurely, before they really understood all their options. They were wrong about their estimates for seed production of the plant itself, and they didn't take into account the poor soil which affected both quality and quantity of seeds they were able to produce."

"I hope the training team goes to Africa soon, Ian, and that they're able to begin building capacity with the locals. I know you've said the farmers are eager to improve their farming techniques, something I'm sure the government supports," Peg offered positively.

"Agreed," Ian nodded. We have a lot of hard work ahead of us between now and their departure, maybe as early as February. It'll continue to be busy until then…both in and out of the labs. I feel bad about not being here for you and the kids."

"Well, don't worry about things around here, Dear," Peg said reassuringly. "I'll do everything I can to keep things rolling. We just need to make sure we explain to the children why you're so busy. I think they'll be proud of you for helping people in faraway Africa. And, if we include them, we can help them see that by sharing their daddy, they are also helping African families…including children. This is actually a rare opportunity for children so young. If they think they are doing their part…they won't feel neglected or left out while you're so busy and less available to spend time with them this winter. We have to be sure we have ongoing family discussions about how things are progressing."

Ian pulled Peg to him and kissed her hair. "Do you know why I love you so much?" he asked. "It's because you are able to take lemons…even troublesome lemons…and make them into lemonade! Thank you, My Dear, Dear Wife, for reminding me that our little ones are bright, caring people…who, of course, would want to be part of this project…want to make a difference. Let's, as you say, make it a family enterprise!"

Ian looked thoughtful and frowned. "We really could use some more help on this project," Ian said. "Unfortunately, there's not money in the budget to hire additional people. That's one of the things that has been keeping me up at night.

I begin to feel like I have to do so much of it myself."

"Hmmm," Peg mused, "I wonder if your dad might be a good person to consult with at this stage of the game? You, know, get a different perspective. Also, what about Jordan? She made it pretty obvious that she was interested in your project…even saying she wanted to become a stowaway on your next trip! Mightn't there be a way to involve her directly in the project? I know you value her expertise and work ethic."

Ian knew he could count on Peggy's common sense and practical suggestions. She actually confirmed some of the things he'd been thinking, himself. He'd thought about talking with his father…he just needed to do it. And involving Jordan was a great idea. Her basic judgment about new directions in plant science was beyond question. It was also well known that the Dean of the College and the Experiment Station Director were encouraging faculty to work across departments. They might be very supportive of her involvement in this project.

He told Peg he would schedule a meeting as soon as possible with Dr. Taylor to see if she would be interested in participating in the Jatropha project. He said he needed to think about what her role might be, and that she might also have some ideas about how she could provide much-needed assistance. Jordan might view an invitation to join the Mozambique project team as a real plus for her career. After all, as an assistant professor, she knew she would have to have well-documented research and several publications in order to get tenure and the promotion.

"By all means try to get her on board…it's probably better to do it before you lose David this spring," Peg suggested. "I know you'll regret losing him after spring graduation. Do you know anything about his future plans? Has he started job hunting yet? Maybe he'll want to return to Texas since that is his home."

"Yup, Peg, he's a Texan," Ian confirmed. "He's been an exceptional grad student. I count my blessings that he chose to follow me here to complete his doctorate. I don't know what I'd have done without his attention to the important details of our work. I have a hunch that he'd really like to get a position at A & M. He'd been seeing someone on the staff there before coming here, and their relationship has endured, even progressed during his time away. But, truthfully, we simply haven't taken the time to discuss his future…which I regret."

"It's never too late to begin that conversation," Peg assured him. "Maybe we could have him over for dinner soon. We might also want to begin thinking about some kind of a farewell celebration when he graduates, especially if his Texas friend and family are coming for his hooding. That would be a nice way to show your appreciation for what he's meant to the Mozambique project."

"Bless you, Mrs. Mahoney!" he said, giving her hand a squeeze. "You never cease to amaze me. Your support and faith in me are truly gifts I don't deserve. Your ideas about how to support my students and colleagues are always so appropriate and welcome. I can certainly understand why your former suitor saw you as the perfect wife for a rising star in the hospitality business. How lucky am I that you chose a stuffy professor like me, instead."

Laughing, she squeezed his hand in return, "Believe me… there are no regrets on my part, Mark Ian Mahoney!"

The two turned out the lights and headed for their bedroom. For the first time in several weeks, a relaxing sleep was about to overtake two, happy Mahoneys.

CHAPTER THIRTEEN

In mid December Jordan awoke one Saturday morning to discover that four or five inches of snow had fallen during the night. That meant she'd better get busy and shovel the driveways. She certainly didn't want Martha to tackle the shoveling. But before she could pull on her boots and ski jacket, the phone rang.

Martha's cheery voice greeted her, "Good morning, Jordan. What a beautiful day! I forgot to tell you that one of the neighbor boys will be along shortly to clear our drives. He mowed the lawn after my son left and has been hired to take care of the snow removal too. I think there's gas in the snow blower in your garage, so that should make quick work of the snow."

"Well, good morning, back, Miss Martha," Jordan matched Martha's cheeriness. "How thoughtful of your son to think ahead and have snow removal all set for us. He seems to have thought of everything to make my stay in his home easy. I noticed the snow blower and was wondering how to use it. That's something I've never done before, but I was ready to try!"

"I just pulled some cinnamon rolls out of the oven. Why don't you come over and join me for a warm breakfast snack?" Martha asked.

Jordan finished buttoning her jacket. "That sounds perfect on a cold wintry morning. I'll be right over."

Soon the two were enjoying a cozy morning visit with warm, gooey cinnamon rolls and mugs of hot chocolate.

"Will you be going to Indiana for the holidays?" Martha inquired.

"No," Jordan said, "although my brother did call and invite me to join him and his wife at her parent's home in Fort Wayne. It was very gracious of them to include me. I have to admit, though, spending both the 24th and 25th with folks I barely know, makes me uncomfortable. I'd sort of feel like a fifth wheel, if you know what I mean."

"But what about your mother? Won't she be alone?" Martha asked carefully, knowing this was a touchy topic for Jordan.

"I really can't say," Jordan said with a combination of hurt and anger in her eyes. "The truth is, I don't even know where she is at this point. Maybe she's not even in the U.S."

"Oh, My Dear, I'm so sorry you've lost touch," Martha said carefully. "I'll be here, too, so maybe we can plan to spend the Christmas together. After all, that's what a grandma and her granddaughter should do!"

"I'd like that very much, Martha. Thanks for thinking of me." Jordan paused a moment, then went on tentatively, "I've…I've…well, I've been less than honest with you, Martha, about my dysfunctional family. If you have the time and don't mind listening to my tale of woe, I'd be relieved to share it with someone who's not apt to be judgmental."

"Well," Martha replied, "the one thing I do have is time… we are snowed in here. Actually, My Dear Jordan, I'd be very interested to find out what it is that's separating your family. Keeping that kind of pain bottled up inside is not very healthy, I'm told. Sometimes it does help to talk about it with someone who cares…and you know I care a great deal about you. Be assured, your story will go no further than this room. Let me get us some more hot chocolate…and this definitely calls for more marshmallows, as well."

Jordan wrapped her hands around the warm mug and gazed into it. "Where to begin…" she faltered. Then looking at Martha directly she said, "One positive thing is that Bill and I are closer than we have ever been. I don't think I was very nice to him when I went off to college. I was more than a little snobbish about playing basketball at a Big Ten school, when he had to settle for a lower-level, college team. I regret it now, and I've told him so."

Martha nodded, "Yes, sibling rivalry can be destructive… especially if the younger one excels in something more than the older one."

Jordan continued, "After Dad was killed on duty, both of us were hurting so much. We were too selfish to even consider Mom's grief. Dad was really the glue that held our family together. We were never perceptive enough to know how much his job worried Mom. She constantly complained that something would surely happen to him while on patrol. We just figured complaining was what wives did. And we really didn't worry too much about Dad…after all, he had always been a police officer, so it was the only life we knew. We were very proud of him.

"Later, after he was gone, I realized how much Mom had resented the fact he had, on numerous occasions, turned down advancements that would have put him behind a desk in an administrative role. But that would never have been his choice. He loved working with people and being able to help those in the community who counted on him."

"I can certainly understand your mom's concern," Martha offered. "We hear way too many sad stories about police officers who die in the line of duty."

Jordan plowed on, "When Dad was killed that rainy night after he'd stopped to assist a stranded motorist, Mom was quick to remind everyone that she had repeatedly predicted that's exactly what would happen."

Martha was quiet for a moment, then she said, "I'm afraid that what your mom was going through is not that uncommon. Often a surviving spouse is just plain angry and frightened to be left alone. So, he or she blames the partner who died…regardless of the circumstances. She must have loved your dad very much to get so angry."

Jordan looked thoughtful, but skeptical. "Well…I suppose that could be true," she said tentatively. "She also turned against his fellow officers and their wives who tried to help. She stopped going to church altogether, even though she never explained why. Maybe she thought God could have… should have…intervened and didn't. On the other hand, she was never the church-goer that Dad was."

"You didn't go to church as a family?" Martha asked.

"No, actually it was always Dad…not she…who took us to Sunday School when we were little," Jordan explained. "Mom always seemed to have some kind of work or project that she just had to do, so she couldn't join us. After his death, Mom said repeatedly that 'trying to be a good Samaritan never did have much pay off.'"

"How sad!" Martha said with feeling. "Church was such a comfort to me when I lost my husband after his last heart attack."

"As I said earlier, my brother and I were dealing with our own grief," Jordan said, "and the loss we were feeling at the time didn't leave us with much empathy for our mother."

"You didn't go home much during that time?" asked Martha.

"No, I am ashamed to say that we didn't," Jordan admitted. "I was too wrapped up in playing basketball and finishing my degree at Purdue with high enough marks to get into a top graduate school to think much about anybody but myself. Then, after my accident, I got behind in my studies and had to work twice as hard to catch up. Going home at the time was a distraction...and dealing with my mom's grief and anger was just more than I could face."

"What about your brother, he was already working, wasn't he?" asked Martha. "Why didn't he go home?"

Jordan tried to explain. "While Bill never felt the same pressure I did to excel academically, he was determined to become a successful high school coach and that took up a lot of time. Besides, he was newly married. When the time came, I didn't even go through commencement ceremonies at Purdue. Instead, I left immediately for Texas."

"How about when you received your doctorate? Did you skip those ceremonies too?" Martha wanted to know. "I remember how proud we were when we saw our only son walk across that stage to receive his hood...the first Webb to have earned a doctoral degree. That was a special day for all of us."

"I can understand how proud you were," Jordan said, "and yes, I did participate in commencement at A & M. In fact, Bill and Maggie came for the ceremony and hosted a lovely dinner for the three of us. They even added a few days for a short holiday, and we took in some of the local historic sights together."

"But how about your mom? Did you invite her to graduation?" Martha asked.

"Yes, of course," Jordan said. "She never even bothered to decline. Instead, she sent me a card that read, 'Congratulations. Enclosed you will find a hundred-dollar bill. Buy yourself a good dinner and a nice bottle of wine.' She signed it with her first name, Evelyn."

"Oh, My Dear Girl," Martha said, patting Jordan's hand. "I can't even imagine how much that must have hurt…after all your hard work and all you'd been through. Does she know about your new position here in East Lansing?"

The beverages got cold, but the conversation continued.

"No, she doesn't!" Jordan said, with thinly-veiled disgust. "You see, my thank-you note came back stamped 'address unknown.' Prior to commencement, Mom had notified my brother and me that that she had packed up some of our belongings and put them in a storage unit near our old home. With the note there was a key for each of us to a locker and notification that storage costs were paid for the next two years. She informed us that she had sold the house and was leaving town."

"But where did she go, if her address was unknown?" asked Martha incredulously.

"During the years after Dad's death, unknown to us, Mom had changed her life completely." Jordan explained. "She gave up the job she loved at a landscaping company. When she sent us the keys she said that she had taken and passed an online course in archeology and that she had quit her job and accepted a position with a 'dig' in Arizona. That was our last known address for her."

"Did she ever have an interest in archeology before?" asked Martha.

Jordan shook her head. "Not that we knew about. In fact, she never even liked to visit museums of any kind. It was always Dad who spent his time off-duty taking us to such places."

"Dear, Dear Jordan," Martha comforted. "What a tremendous burden you have been carrying. Losing not only your father, but…even more tragically…your mother. Add to that the feelings of guilt and anger that continue to plague you. I cannot begin to excuse your mother's actions before or after your father's death, but I do know this. You, My Dear Girl, did nothing wrong. I know you feel guilty about not being there for your mother...but, be assured, that was NOT your role. It was your mother's job to comfort and support you, not the other way around! You were away at college...overwhelmed by all the demands in your life. It really was up to your mom to come to you...to be there for you...to help you deal with your tragic loss. That was especially true after your accident. I don't know your mom, so I can't judge her...she clearly was dealing with her own demons...but I do know that you, My Child, are blameless. I also have to say, your mother did do some things right... look at the beautiful, capable, caring daughter she raised!"

Martha went over and put her arms around Jordan. Holding her tightly, she said, "You, Dear Jordan, are a blessing to me and a magnificent tribute to your wonderful father...and all that was good about your mother. I'm truly sorry she was so troubled, and I hope she finds peace. But for me...having you as my granddaughter is one of the greatest pleasures of my old age!"

Jordan could hold back no longer. Tears spilled out of her eyes and she began to shake with wracking sobs...tears she had been holding inside for too many years to count. Martha held her, rocked her, patted her and whispered, "There, there, let them come...at long last, let them come..."

After some time, with a tear-streaked, mottled face Jordan leaned back, wiped her swollen eyes and gazed at the amazing woman sitting next to her. "I...I..."

"Don't say anything, My Dear," Martha soothed, "you don't have to say a word."

Standing, Jordan caught a glimpse of herself in a wall mirror in the breakfast nook. She burst out laughing. "Oh, my gosh!" she exclaimed. "What a mess! You know, Dear Martha, I feel better than I have felt in...I don't know how long! Thank you for this wonderful gift!" With that she gave Martha a quick hug and grabbed a couple more Kleenex.

"Well," said Martha, "I think you look...lovely! Now, let's talk about Christmas. Since recent Christmases must not have been a lot of fun for you, I think we need to make sure that this year is really memorable! Our family always celebrates on Christmas Eve before attending the candlelight service at church. While going to church doesn't seem to appeal to you, and I wouldn't think of imposing that particular custom on you, we could just have an early dinner and make it something special."

"Wonderful!" exclaimed Jordan, warming to the whole Christmas idea. "What should we have? The agreement is... we do it together. Let's also do a little gift exchange. After all, what is Christmas Eve without a visit from Santa?"

"Of course," agreed Martha. "How about I fix a standing rib roast? I've been wanting an excuse to do that for ages. Is $50 too much for our gift exchange?"

"No, that sounds perfect." Then Jordan added, "Why don't I bring some shrimp cocktail as an appetizer and a cucumber watermelon salad to add some red and green to the menu? Then we can do the potatoes and vegetables together."

"Perfect! I like to plan ahead, so now I can start looking for sales on beef," Martha chirped.

"What a relief," thought Jordan, as she headed home to inspect the work on the drive. She was pleased to see that the neighbor boy had done a good job, and she appreciated that it was relatively easy...thanks to the blower in the garage. "I'll have to ask Martha about paying him," she reminded herself.

As she reflected on their conversation later that day, she

was amazed at how easy it had been to confide in Martha. What a relief it was to finally bare her soul to someone. She felt a sense of calm, relief and closure for something that had been plaguing her for more years than she could remember. Maybe that burden Martha mentioned was part of the reason she had avoided developing a loving relationship with a man. Martha had opened her eyes to a lot of things…had, in one conversation, assuaged her long-standing guilt. Maybe Martha was right about her mother. Maybe her mom's demons had kept her from reaching out to her children…thus keeping them at arms-length and creating a sense of reverse guilt in them! So much to think about…so much to unravel. For now, and in the foreseeable future, though, Jordan was happy with her life as she'd chosen to live it. Perhaps next year she'd think about renewing her credentials to referee Michigan girls' high school basketball games. Perhaps it was time to begin to creep out of her carefully-constructed shell.

Although Jordan had enjoyed officiating high school intermurals as a student, she'd never considered pursuing it as a part-time avocation, until her final two years in Texas. She'd felt the need to start exercising regularly but found little appeal in going to the gym. One night she caught a high school girls' game on the TV news and noticed the officials running up and down the court. "Why couldn't I be in one of those striped shirts?" she'd asked herself.

True to form, she'd wasted no time in locating the requirements for certification, studying them quickly and passing all the informational tests — but not those related to health. But in time, she did trim down – another story – and earned a few coins to purchase some clothes to fit her new figure when, in fact, she got a head start by officiating in a few summer basketball camps held on campus for teens and pre-teen girls.

What a laugh that had produced from her brother, the coach. "A ref? That figures!" he had teased. "One of these days they'll probably hire you to referee men's b-ball games. Won't I hate it if you show up to ref one of my games!"

She smiled as she thought of how her relationship with Bill had improved. Now they both understood that from here on out…it would just be the two of them…together upholding the Taylor name.

CHAPTER FOURTEEN

The twins were excitedly marking days off the calendar until Mimi and Papa would arrive for Christmas in Michigan. Last year's time together was so special — even without Daddy, who was away in Africa. At school they had already begun to make gifts for parents and grandparents. How glad they were to make not only gifts for Daddy and MOMMY, but for THREE sets of grandparents, too! Gifts for the Calhoun grandparents would have to be sent to California this year.

The Gerbers had invited the senior Mahoneys to join them at the farm for the holidays, so everyone was looking forward to their time together. Michael said he just knew G-ma would need them to help decorate Christmas cookies. Ian and Peg had decided to put their tree up a week early this year, so they could enjoy it before leaving Okemos. Thus, they were among the earliest shoppers at the tree farm. Jolly Old Saint Nick, in his bright red suit, was awaiting their arrival.

Much to Santa's surprise, the twins jumped on his lap together. After assuring Santa that they had both been very good this year, they told him that this year they wondered if it would be okay if Santa might bring them a couple of shared gifts. They thanked Santa for the pirate Lego set and Princess Ella doll that he had brought them last year. Then they went on to explain their wish for a new easel with lots of crayons and markers and paper. They were also hoping he would bring them a basketball hoop they could put up outside. Santa had not heard little ones ask him for joint gifts before…and he was surprised and pleased to hear such a request. The man with the white beard nodded, promising he would see what he could do…while the parents looked on in surprise.

Planning was underway for Christmas at the Gerbers. The grownups had agreed to have a "white elephant" swap at the farm instead of exchanging names for gift buying. As a group, they also planned to make a hefty contribution to the local food bank. The Mahoney's second annual trip to Bronner's Christmas Store had been delayed until the 23rd, when the family would be passing Frankenmuth on their way to the farm. The twins had already given Ida a picture book they made, featuring illustrations of things they enjoyed doing with her. A bonus check was also in the mail for her from Peg and Ian. Their Montessori Directress received a box of cheese from the campus dairy store as her present. Last year they had insisted on getting their teacher, Miss Peggy, an angel music box…she was already very special to them! Perhaps that angel had been an omen. They surely couldn't have imagined that this year their former teacher would be their mommy!

The day was sunny when Papa and Mimi arrived from Hilton Head. Fortunately, Big Mike and Kate had come laden with heavy coats and boots, since the forecast predicted cold and snow for Christmas and beyond. Since it had been confirmed that Ian would not be heading to Mozambique in January like last year, the grandparents' stay would be rather short this year.

The house on Ottawa Drive looked festive both inside

and out. The tree included Ian's treasured collection of ornaments from when he was a lad, equally meaningful family ornaments Peg brought with her to their marriage, and the two special ornaments that Mike and Mia had selected last year. The kids were eager to choose new danglers to add to their collection.

The family took off for the Saginaw Valley early on the 23rd…crammed in a 6-person van. When they arrived in Frankenmuth, they stopped for brats and sauerkraut before heading to the Christmas wonderland to find the perfect ornaments. Mia chose a prancing horse this year and Mike, a big bass drum.

All six Mahoneys arrived at the Gerber farm by mid-afternoon and were greeted by a crackling fire in the fireplace, the aroma of hot chocolate on the stove, and yes, the smell of freshly baked Christmas cookies…just as Michael had predicted.

"Thank goodness you're finally here," laughed G-ma. "I've been baking snickerdoodles. The dough is in the refrigerator…but I need helpers to make the cut-outs! You two do such a good job decorating them…I'm so glad you made it!"

"Good," responded the little girl, "Mikey and I hoped you'd save that job for us."

"And licking the frosting bowl is our job too," insisted her twin.

"That's the kind of help we need around here," Papa G laughed merrily.

After stowing snow gear in the mudroom and lugging suitcases and duffle bags upstairs, the adults settled in and began exchanging the latest family news."

"Don't get too comfortable," Rosemary cautioned the adults, "as soon as the boys finish chopping wood for the fireplace, we need to head out and cut down our Christmas tree."

"Hey, Papa G, do we get to ride on the sleigh?" Mia asked hopefully.

"I'm afraid not," their grandfather replied. "There are too many of us to fit into our small cutter. We'll take the big wagon instead, it's already full of fresh straw. And today, I think we'll hitch it to a team of horses instead of the tractor."

"Whoa! What a treat for us!" exclaimed Kate Mahoney. "And with so many strong men on board, we won't need to worry if we get stuck in a snow drift!"

Everyone moved into the mudroom and donned their winter gear. As they went out into the farmyard, they were joined by Peg's three brothers. They had hitched up the horses, who were stomping and ready to go. The young men then helped everyone climb in and get settled, checking to see that all were bundled with blankets amid the straw and making sure the tree cutting tools were on board. Then, the raucous gang set off to find just the right tree.

"There are so many awesome trees…how will we decide?" asked Michael as he pointed to a group of pines.

"Not those! They're too small! Let's keep looking for a bigger one," urged Mia, eager to prolong the adventure.

"No, not that one!" became the theme of the day.

Finally, Papa G, the driver, called, "Okay, You Guys, time-out! You have ten minutes to make a choice! We've got to saw down the tree, tie it to the wagon and get it home before dark."

"Besides, Momma and I are getting cold! Brrrr…." Peg laughed, gleefully. It was the one thing that always seemed to bring the tree-picking to an end.

"Hey!" shouted Michael. "There it is! That's the one!"

Everyone looked at the tree as Mikey jumped off the

wagon and ran to admire a tall, Scotch pine…with his sister right on his heels.

"Yup," he said proudly, "this is it."

Mia walked around the tree slowly…then turning to the folks still in the wagon, she gave a vigorous thumbs-up sign, indicating that they had, indeed, found just the right tree.

JR, Sam and Jake jumped off the wagon and got busy with the chain saw and ropes. They hoisted the big Scotch pine on the back of the wagon, making sure that the ropes held it in place. The bells on the horses' harnesses made a tinkling sound as they headed for home, singing "Jingle Bells," "Over the River" and "You'd Better Watch Out" in the loudest voices they could muster. The wagon rolled toward home, just as twilight was beginning to darken the sky.

After unloading the tree, everyone warmed themselves by the fire. Soon the Christmas revelers were ready for an early supper of beef stew, biscuits and fruit salad, followed by a huge platter of Rosemary's assorted Christmas cookies…cookies she'd been baking all week. While the tree was being set up in the family room, lights strung and decorations hung, the twins busied themselves stringing chains of popcorn and cranberries, which they, in turn draped around the boughs.

After stowing the Christmas ornament crates and picking up pine needles, the family dropped into chairs, couches, and onto to floor to admire the tree. It was a beautiful sight with twinkling lights, tons of ornaments, garlands galore and a bright shining star on top. Tired from a very busy day…everyone decided to turn in early. They all knew that tomorrow would be another big day.

Early the next morning, Ian and his father joined the four male Gerbers, as they led the way to the barn to feed the animals and do the morning chores. Everyone appreciated the hearty breakfast of French toast, bacon and eggs that the grandmothers had prepared. They all ate with gusto and especially enjoyed the box of grapefruit and oranges that had unexpectedly arrived from Florida.

All the men cleared out, except – that is – for young Michael, who opted to join in the decorating of star, bell, Christmas tree and snowman cookies — plus a few sheep and a couple of reindeer, for good measure. Kate was assigned to decorate the mantle with holly and pine cones and to create a centerpiece for the dining room table. Peg's job was to line up a dozen colorful tins to hold the cookies slated to be given away later that day. After all the cookies were finally decorated, Mia and Mike finally got to lick the frosting bowl. Of course, there was as much frosting on lips, cheeks, hands and aprons as there was on the cookies…but that's Christmas, after all.

After chores, Sam had run out to do some last-minute shopping for his mother. When he returned, he had several large pizzas to go with the veggie salad that was waiting in the refrigerator for lunch. After such a big breakfast, it was surprising that anyone was hungry, but the pizzas and salad were demolished in record time by this rather boisterous family.

After lunch, the "girls" began to pack up cookies to deliver to several nursing homes in the area, while the "boys" settled in to watch a couple of college basketball games.

Upon their return, Mia was eager to tell the guys about their visits to the elderly in the nursing homes. "They were so glad to see us," she said enthusiastically. "They asked a lot of questions and told stories of Christmas in the olden days. I'm so glad that we could help them have a Merry Christmas. And guess what, Mikey, they really thought our cookies were beautiful! They even gave me these chocolate

Santas to thank us!"

Dinner was soon ready. After downing a comfort meal of baked macaroni and cheese, Caesar salad, and French bread, everyone prepared for the Christmas eve at church. They were attending the early children's service.

After settling into two full pews, they Gerbers and Mahoneys sang the opening ode, "Joy to the World." The twins watched in delight as youngsters performed the traditional story of Mary, Joseph, shepherds, angels, wise men and, of course, Baby Jesus. They were pleased when they and other children were invited to come up front and join the performers in the finale…the singing of "Away in a Manager."

This service like most on that special night, ended when everyone in the church chain-lit candles, and held them high while singing the closing hymn, "Silent Night." After the service, they all joined Gerber friends, neighbors and fellow church members for hot cider and a cookie or two before stepping out into the freezing night and heading to the farm.

"That was truly a lovely service," remarked Big Mike on the drive home. "One can just imagine the thousands of churches around the world who are celebrating the birth of the Christ Child in much the same way we are, here in America. Hopefully, on this one night we can join hands in peace and accept that we are all brothers and sisters…with one Father."

"Amen!" the others agreed.

"The twins began to sing quietly from their booster seats, "I love You, Lord Jesus, look down from the sky and …." Who knows, their special guardian angel just might be looking down from above and will stay by their bedside "…til morning is nigh…"

When they got home, Christmas carols were played in the background as the children hung their stockings, set out treats for Santa and the reindeer and wrote him a cheery note. Soon little eye-lids began to droop…signaling tooth-brushing, prayers, one more Christmas story and tucking of kids into warm, cozy sleeping bags. Surely visions of sugar plums would soon be dancing in their heads.

The adults stretched out on overstuffed chairs and couches and chatted, while waiting for the children to fall asleep. Then they arranged gifts under the tree and in the children's stockings. They were sure to include a thank you note from Santa next to the plate of cookie crumbs and reindeer footprints left by the fireplace. Finally, the weary adults followed the children's lead and headed off for their own long winter's nap.

On Christmas morning, Michael and Mia raced into their parents' bedroom at the crack of dawn. They could smell coffee brewing downstairs…and egg casserole baking in the oven.

"Come on, Mommy, Daddy!" the twins said as one. "We have to see if Santa came. They grabbed their parents' hands and dragged them out of the bedroom, barely allowing them time to grab their robes and slippers. Racing down the stairs, their shrieks would have awakened anyone still lucky enough to be dreaming.

Of course, the others had been up long before them. They heard the Gerber men coming in the back door after taking care of the animals, while the grandmothers worked busily in the kitchen.

"He came! Santa came! Look at all the presents!" shouted the kids with over-the-top enthusiasm.

"And look!" Mia said, "Santa left us a note!"

"And the reindeer left footprints in the sugar we left for them!" Michael added. "And Santa ate all the cookies!"

"Can we open our stockings, Daddy?" Mia begged.

"Please?" added Michael.

"Hold on, you two," cautioned their dad. "You can look everything over, but we have to wait for everyone to get here, before we open anything."

"Okay, Daddy," Mia said, "but make them HURRY!"

To their great surprise the boys and girls of all ages would have something to open before breakfast. On the sly, Rosemary and Kate had filled identical red stockings for all the adults. They were stuffed with candy canes, tangerines, popcorn balls, sugar free chewing gum, shiny quarters, new ink pens, chocolate Santas, lottery tickets…and even a few chunks of coal, in some. The twins had many of those surprises in their stockings, as well as holiday stickers and red and green markers. After opening stockings amid laughter and exclamations, everyone pitched in and fixed his or her own breakfast: egg casserole, pumpkin roll, oatmeal, yogurt, fruit, bagels…quite the feast.

In spite of the decision of the adults to forget about real presents this year, there were still a lot of wrapped gifts under the tree – mostly from out-of-town relatives and friends. The children were delighted to unwrap books, new pajamas, a couple of games and some school clothes. They began to wonder if Santa had forgotten them, when they saw a gift in a large gift bag behind the tree. Could it be? The children ripped off the bag – and there, was the most beautiful easel they had ever seen! It had a marker board on one side and a chalkboard on the other and clamps to hold chart paper on both sides!

"I love it! It's perfect!" exclaimed the twins.

They then noticed another big box that the easel bag had hidden earlier. Opening it, Michael and Mia excitedly pulled out chalk, markers, paints and many other art supplies, including several pads of chart paper. They were so engrossed in the pile of art supplies, that they didn't even notice Uncle JR, when he brought in a tall, wrapped box.

"Hey, Kids," puffed Uncle JR, "look what I found in the garage. It wasn't there last night, so I wonder how it got there."

The children abandoned their art supplies and ran over to the big box. They began pulling off the big, red bow and ripping the paper; hoping this strangely-shaped box might possibly hold their other Christmas request.

"Santa left it there," Michael declared. "This box was way too big to bring down the chimney, so he must have put it in the garage, instead."

They pulled off the last shred of colorful paper and asked Daddy to use the scissors to cut the tape holding the box shut. As he slowly did so, they jumped up and down with excitement shouting, "Hurry, Daddy, hurry!"

Inside the box was an adjustable, stand-alone, solid metal post with a child-sized hoop attached. There were even two basketballs in the box.

"He did it!" shouted Michael. "He brought us a basketball hoop!"

Grabbing one of the basketballs and bouncing it on the carpet, Mia added, "I knew he'd do it! It's just what we wanted!"

Michael turned to the admiring crowd and announced, "I really want to play basketball and be just like Miles Bridges, and now I can!"

"We both do!!" piped up Mia. "Mr. Paul from our school is going to teach us. Mommy says he used to play in college…and he got paid for playing after that…so he really knows all about it!"

"Don't forget, Daddy's friend, Miss Jordan, played basketball, too," reminded her brother.

Sam grabbed the other basketball and made a quick chest

pass to Jake who snagged it and feigned a layup. "Guess what, you two," Sam sneered. "All three of your uncles played basketball in high school, too…and we still play whenever we can…so you'll have lots of coaches to help you learn!"

"Wow," Michael said with unabashed admiration. "Can we play now?"

Jake rolled the ball to his nephew. "I don't think G-ma will let us play in the house," he said, indicating the tree, lamps, pictures, cups of hot chocolate. Then, in a stage whisper he said to both kids, "Come here." He leaned down and put his hands on their shoulders. "Maybe we can slip out into to the garage later and shoot a few hoops, what do you say?"

"Yea! Yes! Can we go now?" was the bouncingly eager response.

Papa G raised his hands for attention and indicated the Christmas tree. "Hold on a minute. I think we grownups have a few gifts to unwrap…how about we do that first?"

The kids ran to their parents and settled beside them on the couch. "Let's see what's in them," Mia agreed.

The adults took turns picking a "white elephant" gift from under the tree. Mommy had told them that this might be a little boring for kids, since the grown-ups would be acting silly and admiring the old stuff hidden in the beautifully-wrapped packages. They watched though, trying to be "grown up" themselves. But, just when they starting eyeing their art supplies and basketball hoop longingly, Daddy came to their rescue. He pulled from behind his back an unwrapped surprise gift – a video of the latest Disney movie they hadn't seen. With a nod from their parents, they trotted off to the living room to watch it. Meanwhile, the others laughed and teased as they traded gifts back and forth… each trying to snag the best "treasure." Finally, each had a humorous gift to keep: a tattered old Superman comic book, a half-burned Christmas candle, a pair of purple bed socks with a missing toe in each, a roll of green toilet tissue, a jar of colored soaps, an orange necktie, a can of rusty nails. You name it, and someone ended up with it. It was great fun.

After everyone had a good laugh, it was time for lunch. Since everyone confessed to having already indulged in too many sweets at holiday parties, they'd decided to pass on the traditional Christmas dinner. Instead, they opted for leftover shrimp cocktail, hot ham sandwiches, hash-brown-potato casserole, orange and pineapple salad and, of course, Jesus's birthday cake. What a mountain of goodness that was — alternating layers of dark red and white cake covered with oodles of white fluffy frosting. There was even a pretty lighted candle on top. The twins insisted on singing "Happy Birthday."

"We forgot the balloons," they whispered to each other in distress, while overfilling their mouths with the sweet, frothy confection.

After lunch and a few basketball scrimmages in the garage, the uncles departed. JR went to join his fiancée, Lindsay, for Christmas dinner with her family; Sam headed back to Midland to finish work on a court case he was prosecuting; and Jake left to join several high school buddies. The pals were making a surprise visit to a former teacher who was in the Rehab Center recovering from a broken arm and leg. The poor fellow had taken a fall while placing the star on the tree in his home a few days before Christmas. They wanted to tell him that they would be taking down the tree for him and his wife – to make sure he wouldn't try anything foolish while still in his casts.

The remaining adults tidied up the kitchen and moved to the family room, where they gathered up scraps of paper and ribbon and put them in the recycling bin. Once the place was relatively neat; Papa G went out to check on the animals, and Ian and his folks headed upstairs to make the beds and finally take showers. The twins retired to the couch in the living room and began looking through their new books – soon, they both fell asleep.

Peg followed her mom to the breakfast nook for some private time. After agreeing Christmas had been a huge success, and chatting about their respective plans for the week, Rosemary leaned forward and looked seriously at her daughter.

"Honey," Rosemary began tentatively, "I wanted to ask you if everything is okay at home? You haven't seemed to be yourself since you arrived. I'm wondering what happened to my happy, always-smiling Margaret Ann?"

"Oh, dear, was it that obvious?" Peg responded, horrified.

"No, Peggy Ann, nothing was obvious. You were cheerful, helpful and engaging, as always," Rosemary smiled, patting her daughter's hand. "But I thought I caught a frown or two, when you thought no one was looking."

"Leave it to you to notice," Peg sighed. "You're really something, Mom."

"Is everything okay between you and Ian?" she asked. "Now that I think about it, he seemed 'not quite himself,' either."

"The truth is, Mom, we're always so tired. We both have growing responsibilities at work, church projects are demanding and the twins are great...but with school, extracurricular activities, projects and now sports we feel like we have to keep running just to stay even! There's never any time for US! We've only had two meals without the kids, since our honeymoon; once when we hosted Jordan and Paul and once at Paul's apartment."

"I remember you told me about those dinner dates.

Wasn't that first dinner when Jordan acted so strangely?" Peg's mom asked.

"Yes," Peg confirmed, "...add worrying about our friends to the increasing list of stressors."

"I have to admit, Peggy Dear, I was afraid that this might happen...even with Mrs. Harding's priceless help." Rosemary paused, then looked directly into Peg's eyes. "Peg, please listen to what I have to say. You MUST make time for yourself and your husband to nurture the love that brought you together. That means, regardless of everything else... spending time alone together has to be your first priority!"

"But . . ." her daughter began to protest.

"There are no 'buts' about it, Margaret Ann," Rosemary interrupted. "Believe me, I know how hard it can be to find time to be together. Remember, your dad and I had four of you kids! It's true instead of a fulltime job, I job-shared after you and JR arrived, but we had a farm to run...which was a second fulltime job for both your dad and me. I couldn't quit work, since making the mortgage payments on the farm was quite a load for us back then. We couldn't afford expensive date nights, either, so we had to get creative in order to spend a couple of hours by ourselves."

"Like, what did you do? I don't remember you being gone that much," Peg asked.

Rosemary laughed. "Well, we set up a babysitting exchange with our neighbors who also had young ones, so we didn't have to pay for a sitter. Then, in the summer we took a blanket and thermos of lemonade and went to listen to a free concert in the park or we went for a hike and a picnic by the lake, or we drove to Frankenmuth to visit the museum, or any number of other outings. Like I said, when it's a priority, you have to get creative. Most often, though, after you were all in bed, we'd just sit in rockers on the porch and talk. It's not where you are that matters, it's making a commitment to carve out time to be together that's important."

"You know, Mom, you're right," Peggy admitted. "Lately, once the kids are in bed, Ian retires to his computer to do a hour or two of extra research, while I sit at the kitchen table writing lesson plans or reviewing student work. Sometimes we're like passing ships in the night…hardly acknowledging each other. Then, we're so tired, we literally collapse into bed. It's funny how easy it is to fall into that routine."

Rosemary nodded her head knowingly, "Don't add guilt to your list of stressors, Dear. What you're describing many couples experience…including your dad and me. The trick is to pledge to each other that you will make the time to be together…plan it on the calendar, if you have to. The truth is, unless you are loved and supported by each other…neither of you will be able to love or support others."

Peg shook her head in admiration, "You're really a gem, do you know that, Momma? You've really given me a lot to think about. In my heart, I know what you're saying is true. But it's so easy to make excuses for not doing the 'couple thing' when you're feeling overwhelmed. Truthfully, both Ian and I miss our time alone. We loved our seemingly-endless together-time in Italy…and now that almost seems like a distant memory. I guess the fact that we never really dated much before we were married…could be part of the problem."

Again, Rosemary nodded, "I'll admit, that was a concern for us, too; but your friendship was so strong and value-based that we pushed our uneasiness aside. Well, that's it, then! You're going right back on my prayer list…not that you've ever been off it…but now I'm going to focus on praying for your together time! Not to worry, My Dear Daughter, you and Ian both want the same things…I know you'll figure this one out. Now, let's see if we can scare up something to feed the hoards." With that, Rosemary got up and headed to the refrigerator.

For dinner, there was homemade French onion soup, an assortment of MSU's Dairy Club cheeses with crackers, leftover salads and casseroles and loads of Christmas cookies… enough to satisfy any number of hungry souls.

That night, after the children were tucked into their sleeping bags and prayers had been said, Mia surprised her parents by saying, "Daddy and Mommy, do you remember the boxes we filled with stuff for the kids in Africa? I sure hope our presents helped them have a merry Christmas, too…just like ours!"

"Oh, yeah," added her brother, who had forgotten all about the Christmas boxes they had assembled after Thanksgiving. "I picked out those trucks and superhero coloring books. I bet they liked those! And I know they liked the soccer balls…everybody likes soccer."

"You two are really special, you know that?" their dad asked. "Mommy and I are so proud of you. Not only do you make us happy, every single day, but you made some kids…halfway around the world…have a happy Christmas this year, too. Good night, my little Christmas elves."

With that, their parents kissed them both and gave them one, additional hug each. As they headed downstairs, the couple smiled and nodded to each other, recalling that Saturday after Thanksgiving. The four of them had gone shopping to find gifts to fill two Samaritan Purse boxes they'd picked up at the church. The boxes' final destination had been rural Mozambique, and the gifts were to be distributed among children in the small village that had welcomed their father earlier that year. What made Peg and Ian really smile was remembering how the youngsters had insisted on using the allowance money they had stashed in their banks all year to buy something each of them wanted. After talking between themselves, they had announced that they planned to use their money to fill the gift boxes…it was, they informed their parents, exactly what each of them really wanted to buy with their money.

Both Ian and Peg were thinking the same thing, "How amazing these little tykes are. Even at their young age they have discovered that it truly is 'more blessed to give than receive!'" And as their parents…they could not be prouder!

CHAPTER FIFTEEN

The return trip to Okemos was uneventful, thanks to the success of the highway crews in getting rid of the patches of black ice that had terrorized travelers the day before. Everyone was happy to have a rather restful day to unwind and plan for the final days of the Senior Mahoneys' stay in Michigan.

After taking a day to dismantle the shedding Christmas tree and make a few phone calls to confirm plans for the next day, the gang on Ottawa Drive were ready to take advantage of their few remaining vacation days. As it turned out, most members of the family had specific plans for the following day. Only Peg chose to remain at home.

During breakfast of what promised to be a busy six or seven hours, each family member reported on his/her plans for the day. Ian and his dad were going to the office to discuss Ian's upcoming meetings and issues related to the Mozambique project. They also had a lunch date at the International Center with Jordan. She had promised to take Big Mike on a tour of the horticulture offices and labs after lunch.

The twins were scheduled for a play date at the Allen home. Young BJ was eager to have his friends see his new Tommy the Train and play with his toy farm and zoo. Mia was excited to see BJ, of course, but she was all smiles and rather secretive about what she and "Auntie Jo," would also be doing. Jodie was looking forward to spending time with Mia, although she knew she would have to lure her away from the Tommy Train and farm/zoo play-mania. Mia enjoyed playing with both boys and girls...and she loved trucks and trains...probably because she and her brother had been sharing all their toys since birth! Jodie, however, missed playing with her niece who lived up north. She liked doing special "girly" things, and BJ just wasn't interested... so...Mia would be her "girly" friend for the day.

Kate spoke up next, "I'm having lunch with two old friends from here. After lunch at the Kellogg Center, we're going to visit the new condo of one of the gals. She tried living with her daughter in Vermont, but that didn't work out so well. Her place is in a newly-completed, three-story building with only twelve units. It's near an adult care center, which appeals to her, since her daughter is so far away...and...as we all have to admit...we just aren't getting any younger." She laughed merrily.

Everyone turned to the only silent one at the table, "And you, Miss Peggy, what's up your sleeve? How do you plan to spend the day?" teased her father-in-law.

"Nothing all that exciting," was the reply. "I plan to stay right here and do something I've been putting off for the last couple of months...sort the twins' clothes and identify things they've outgrown. I'm going to donate them to the chapel's coat drive or include them in a package of children's things we're sending to Mozambique."

All the travelers were on their way by mid-morning. Kate helped Peg clean up the kitchen before showering and getting dressed for her outing. She and her friends had had minimal contact through the years, so she was hungry for updates on their families and retirement activities. Let's be honest, she was also eager to share pictures of her grandchildren and talk about her new daughter-in-law and their extended Michigan family, the Gerbers.

Once alone, Peg relaxed with a second cup of coffee before attacking her task. It was hard to believe how much the "munchkins" had grown since last winter. Michael might take after Papa, a bigger guy than his lanky dad. And Mia – well that was hard to predict. Her birth mother was quite petite from what she could tell from the photos in the kids' rooms, but Mia's legs seemed to have stretched out in the past six months. Both five-year-olds had quickly out-grown their shoes. She hummed as she went about her work, glad to have this "free" time to tackle a task that ordinarily would have been postponed.

After arriving at Ian's office, the two men fell into easy, comfortable conversation. They were glad to have some one-on-one time to really talk. Mike, after learning more about his son's fluid situation at work, was thoughtful – but, as usual, a creative problem-solver. Although Mike was a competent bench scientist, he'd have to admit that outreach, marketing and human resource development were more his forte. It was not surprising that he had some ideas about how to negotiate with administrators to gain support for Jordan's role in Ian's project. Back in the day, Mike, himself, had secured funding for several interdepartmental projects. He couldn't help recalling how he had spear-headed two such projects. One was the winter storage of apples and another was the branding of a new beverage (a combination non-alcoholic wine/sparkling grape juice).

"Dad," his son said, shaking his head. "You never fail to amaze me with your people and your problem-solving skills. I never knew about the apple storage and wine/grape juice projects. What are you doing now to keep that logistical mind of yours challenged?"

"Not very much, I'm afraid…that bothers me," Mike responded. "You can only play so much golf, Ian. While I still enjoy the game, playing 18 holes on a different course each Tuesday is really not what I'd like to be doing."

"How about Mom," Ian probed, "is she happy living in a planned community? How does she keep busy and challenged?"

"Well you know your mom," his dad smiled. "She participates in several women's groups and signs up for local classes. In fact, she just learned how to make bead jewelry, of all things. We both think the move to Carolina was a good thing. I have to say, we don't miss all that winter shoveling and slippery driving. Our weather is really quite pleasant from November to March. Summer can be pretty hot and humid, though." Mike laughed. "I probably sound conflicted, I know. I guess you could say there are trade-offs. But, in all honesty, I think that your mom misses her friends from here and Washington. And, of course, the thing we both miss the most…is spending time with the four of you! Our grandchildren are growing up way too fast!"

"Yeah, I can see that. We miss you guys, too!" Ian agreed. "I know you loved traveling overseas…and you always had so many international friends. Have you met any folks from other countries, since you've had a chance to get settled?"

Mike nodded. "Actually, Son, we recently had an interesting couple move in next door. They've spent the past decade in Japan, where he was associated with GM. His name is Bert and he's from Michigan, but his wife is Japanese. While in Japan, he became interested in Japanese biofuels that were being used to power Japanese vehicles. He still tries to keep up with his language skills by speaking Japanese at home and subscribing to a number of Japanese publications. His wife, who speaks English quite well, actually worked in agriculture at a university there. It was while he was attending a seminar on biofuels at the university, that he actually met his wife. She's teaching Kate the art of flower arranging and Japanese cooking. Sushi and sashimi are becoming a regular part of my diet, and I'm really getting quite proficient with chop sticks!!!!"

You could almost see the wheels turning in Ian's head. He had been frustrated with his inability to learn as much as he wanted to know about the Japanese work on bio-fuels…especially what they were doing with Jatropha. Do you suppose that these neighbors might have a way to connect with Japanese agronomists working on projects similar to his own?

"Son," said the fellow who might be able to add mind reader to his many other skills, "I'd be willing to discuss your issue with Bert and Yoshimi and see if they might be able to dig up some publications or government reports that would shed light on what's happening over there regarding biofuel investigations. Yoshimi might well have contacts at the university who were involved with such research. Bert's always eager to learn new things…and Yoshimi has been struggling with retirement, after leaving her successful academic career in Japan. I have to admit, I miss those heated but friendly debates I used to have with campus colleagues, myself. My neighbors just might spark my "academic debate" gene that has become a little dormant, of late."

After glancing at his watch, Ian stood and the two men headed to the International Center to meet Jordan, who was certain to be on time. Sure enough, Jordan was waiting to greet them in the lobby of the Center, a favorite lunch spot for Mike when he had worked at MSU. Jordan looked both professional and perky in her bright red wool coat.

"Hi, Jordan," Ian said, smiling, "this is my father, Michael

Mahoney…Big Mike, as most people call him."

Jordan reached out her hand and took Mike's in her firm grip. "How do you do, sir. This is a pleasure I've been anticipating since I made the connection between you and your son. I heard a lot about your outstanding leadership at Washington during my time in College Park. I also heard that you were honored as a 'Fellow' by our national association last year. Congratulations!"

Returning her handshake, Mike responded, "Thank you, Professor Taylor. It was both surprising and humbling to get that award…especially since it came from my peers. I have to say, I've heard a lot of great things about some of your work, too." He laughed. "I can't seem to stop reading about current research in the many ag journals that still clutter our coffee table. Tell me, what's the verdict on 'freezing' the age of ornamental grass at its prime?"

Surprised and flattered, Jordan responded eagerly, "Amazingly positive. Actually, we're quite close to solving our grass-aging problem. We're actually starting several five-year field trials this spring, thanks to two contacts I made with landscapers in November at a show in Grand Rapids."

Mike nodded his approval, thinking that the field trials would most likely keep her in East Lansing for awhile… surely long enough for her to get tenure and promotion. That would bode well for Ian's intention to involve her in the Department of Energy study.

The trio ordered and enjoyed lunch, while the men told stories about their holiday at the farm. She was pleased to hear about the twins' interest in learning to play basketball and commented that the "white elephant exchange" must have been a hoot.

Then the conversation turned to her Christmas activities. Ian recalled that she and her neighbor planned to have

Christmas Eve dinner together before Mrs. Webb went to church. Jordan reported that dinner was "smashing," especially the English dessert Martha made with special ingredients that her son's wife had sent from England.

"I'll bet it was a well-aged fruit cake soaked in lots of brandy or rum," suggested an all-knowing Mike.

"Sorry, you're wrong this time!" Jordan laughed. "It was a special raspberry and kiwi trifle. It even had Birds' custard in it, made from a packet of mix that had accompanied the recipe. But…just as we were about to have coffee and some authentic English Christmas favors, there was a knock at the door. It was the neighbor who clears the driveway. He wanted to report that he'd be shoveling the drive first thing the next morning, since it would be pointless to do the job before the street was cleared."

She paused, and the men guessed that her story was completed. Not so!

She took a deep breath and a strange look came over her face, as she continued, "He went on to say that he and his buddies had decided to shovel a path from all their neighbors' homes to the corner where the church was located, so that folks who wanted to attend Christmas Eve service could walk. It was really very thoughtful of them…I knew Martha had been looking forward to the service for several days."

"I hesitated a minute before I told Martha about the cleared path to the church. I knew how important attending a Christmas Eve service was to the Webb family, but… I hadn't planned on attending myself." She blushed and looked at Mike. "I have to admit, I really don't believe in the mythology of religion, myself…and avoid it whenever possible. However, I also knew Martha could not venture down the newly-shoveled paths by herself. So, I gulped and announced that we'd better forget about the dishes, pull on our boots and head out to catch the early Christmas Eve service. After all, how bad could it be? There were sure to be lots of familiar songs, and who can seriously object to children in bathrobes depicting shepherds? So off we went. I really did enjoy giving 'Grandmother Martha' her Christmas wish. Surprisingly…I actually enjoyed it, myself…or at least, I enjoyed watching Martha enjoy it."

While the men wanted to applaud her decision, they merely smiled and nodded in agreement. They really didn't know how to respond to such a story.

In the silence that followed, Jordan found herself wondering if she should bring up concerns she had been having lately about the value of her research. Although the end result would be good news for homeowners who wouldn't have replacement costs of ornamental grasses, it could, in turn, mean less business and a financial loss for growers and landscapers. When compared to the projected outcomes related to Ian's work, it all seemed rather trivial. Increasing the GNP of a developing nation and providing a more sustainable source for biodiesel production seemed a lot more meaningful than ornamental grasses!

Ian settled her dilemma by broaching that very subject, himself. "Jordan, I know you've mentioned that you might be interested in working with us on Jatropha…are you truly willing to join out group on a part-time basis? I know you have your own field trials starting soon…and I wouldn't want our work to delay your research, but we'd be grateful to have you on board."

The young woman could hardly contain her excitement, "My friend, I thought you'd never ask! Of course, I want to help you in any way I can! I've been having second thoughts about the long-term value of my weed research. I'm not ready to abandon it, because I believe "freezing grasses" could have benefits beyond their decorative use, but I do think that I need to broaden my research focus. I'm quite sure I could continue with my field trials…and still find time for some part-time collaboration with your group. Do you think that the administration and Department of Energy folks would agree to broaden my research focus?"

Ian expressed his optimism that they could set up an inter-department agreement. He went on to explain that his father had coordinated a couple of interdepartmental projects, himself, and had shared some of the strategies that had worked for him to get similar partnerships approved. With luck their scheduled meeting next week might just pave the way for a brand new initiative.

"While I was ready to beg to join you in Mozambique… as another grad assistant," she laughed as they stood up from their table, "working directly with you here on campus sounds even better. Thanks for lunch, Ian." They left the International Center and headed over to the Plant and Soil Sciences building to begin the promised tour of the Horticulture Department.

At dinner that evening, all the Mahoneys were eager to report on their days' activities. Michael told everyone about all the fun he'd had playing older brother to little PJ…and that PJ had some really cool trains and trucks. Mia stated that she was officially PJ's "big sister," too…and that Auntie Jo had taught her to knit. She proudly presented Mommy and Mimi with potholders she had made all by herself that very afternoon!

Ian and Mike were excited to tell everyone about their meeting with Jordan and how hopeful they were that the proposed partnership would work out.

Kate told everyone how much she had enjoyed spending time with her friends and sharing photos of grandchildren.

She loved seeing Marilyn's new condo and hearing how happy she was to be back in familiar territory. Marilyn had re-established her membership with her Lansing area P.E.O. Chapter (Philanthropic Education Organization), through which she had met several new friends. Kate went on to say that she was sorry she had never joined that group, which supported college scholarships for women and seemed to have chapters everywhere.

Peg chimed in that her mother was a P.E.O. member and often talked about how nice it was for women who moved from place to place, since there were, indeed, chapters all across the country that eagerly welcomed newcomers. Peg added that someday when the twins were older, she, too, might join a local chapter. She also announced, proudly, that her day had been very productive. She had filled four boxes with shoes and clothes that she found in the back of the children's closets and in the basement. Some of those outfits were for toddlers she told them while smiling at her husband. Ian had actually moved clothes from Texas that the children had already outgrown. She reported how delighted Pastor Becky was to get them. The collection for Mozambique was almost ready to be shipped. Michael and Mia clapped their hands, cheered by the fact that their old clothes would become "new" for kids across the globe.

It was a tired bunch of Mahoneys, who soon retreated to their respective bedrooms, climbed into warm beds and reflected on how lucky they all were to have a loving family who celebrated each others' joys, shared their concerns and surrounded each other with love and acceptance.

CHAPTER SIXTEEN

The elder Mahoneys were packed and ready to leave for the airport. As Mike and Ian lugged suitcases out to the car, Mike said to Ian, "I heard back from Bert. He was very interested in what you are doing with Jatropha. He assured me that both he and Yoshimi would be excited to do a bit of investigation into Japanese biofuel research. He said he didn't know what they might be doing with Japtropha, per se, but he would be willing to chat with Yoshimi and the two of them would see what they could find out."

"That's great news, Dad!" Ian said, throwing the last of the bags into the back of the car. "Just having a connection with someone who might be able to provide some insight into what the Japanese are doing…and perhaps a contact or two in Japan would be invaluable. Once, again, you have come through for me, Dad. I'm also going to take your advice about the upcoming meeting. I'll be meeting with my team early this week, and I'll be sure to stress the importance of impressing the brass."

Mike nodded, "I know it sounds a bit old fashioned, but I also know that in a meeting where you are requesting financial support and program change, it's important for all players to be well prepared and professional in their presentation. It wouldn't hurt to have our Peggy provide some of her yummy scones for the meeting, either. I've found that sugar almost always sweetens even the toughest negotiations."

"That's a great idea, Dad, I'll ask her if she has time to make them before Thursday," Ian agreed.

Just then they were joined by a bundled Kate and a shivering threesome of Peg, Michael and Mia. Hugs and kisses, thanks, and promises to see one another soon were exchanged. As the car pulled out, Peg and the children remained in the driveway, waving until their dad and grandparents were out of sight.

"I'm going to miss Mimi and Papa," Mia said sadly. "I don't want them to go."

"I know, Sweetheart," comforted her mother, drawing both children close as they headed to the house, "but we'll see them again, before you know it. Those two can't stay away from you for long."

"Yeah," agreed Michael, "and Papa said they would Facetime us as soon as they get home…and that's almost like having them here."

"You're right, Mikey," said Peg, "and they both are loaded with presents you made them and pictures you created that will soon be hung all over their house…reminding them of their two favorite grandkids!"

"Mooooom," Mikey protested, "we're their ONLY grandkids!"

All three laughed as they hurried into their warm house. The kids headed to their rooms, and Peg was off to clean up the kitchen. She hummed as she thought about how different this Christmas had been…her first as a wife and a mother. She could not have imagined how full her life would become in just one, short year.

Ian needn't have worried about his staff, as it all turned out. At their planning meeting on Monday, team members, themselves, brought up attire for their upcoming meeting.

Even "casual" Christian mentioned that he planned to wear the new sport coat he had purchased for Christmas services this year. Kevin and Jay ran through the Power Point they had put together, which described their plans for training farmers in Mozambique. Ian had also prepared a Power Point outlining the status of Jatropha genetic research. Christian, Dana, David and Jordan joined the others in offering suggestions on how the slide shows could be enhanced. Ian then went over the proposed agenda, and each member of the team offered talking points for his/her area of expertise. Finally, after some debate, much discussion, and a bit of tweaking, all were satisfied that they were ready to submit their agenda to Department Chairman, Harry Wagner, who would be running Thursday's meeting. They left feeling exhausted but exhilarated by the possibilities the meeting offered.

The next morning, Ian met with Dr. Wagner to go over the proposed agenda. Wagner asked several questions and suggested Ian and his team address one or two points they had not considered. After approving the agenda and the logistics for the meeting (Ian promising to bring snacks), they concluded their discussion.

On Thursday, everyone arrived at the conference room in plenty of time for the meeting. Ian had found his gray suit and a fresh, cream-colored shirt on the bed following his shower that morning. Peg had, indeed, baked fresh scones and sent a basket of them along with a tray of grapes, crackers and cheese for the meeting. Fresh coffee and water was also arranged on the side table.

The team looked spiffy that morning and had all their notes ready. Right on time, the Chair escorted the Dean of the College, James Wilson, and the Director of the Experiment Station, Martin Schwartz, into the conference room.

Both men were shivering from their brief walk in the January weather. After hanging their coats on the coat rack, Ian introduced his team to the administrators. Then everyone grabbed a plate of goodies and coffee or bottles of water, then found places around the conference table.

Once everyone was settled, Wagner distributed agendas and briefly reviewed the topics they would be discussing: the USAID training program for farmers in Mozambique, the Energy Department Jatropha genetic research project that Ian had brought with him from Texas and possible changes and new directions for the project in the future.

Kevin and Jay began the discussion, using their Power Point to outline their teaching-learning plans aimed at increasing the agricultural output of farmers in Mozambique. The topics included basic agricultural practices…most of which were used regularly in the United States…but which were new to rural, independent farmers in many parts of Africa. Jay explained that African farmers needed to improve their basic knowledge and practices, if they were to make their farming profitable. Kevin emphasized the importance of providing hands-on supervision, so the new skills would be used appropriately and retained after the training sessions.

Jay went on to explain that what was unique about their training program was its tiered teaching approach. With the help of the US Agricultural Attaché assigned to the region, a group of the most respected local farmers (those identified as quick learners and key influentials would be identified. They would receive extensive training – not only in agricultural methods, but teaching and mentoring, as well. Then, each would, in turn, help teach his neighbors, monitor their practices and be available to assist, as necessary. The "teaching" farmers would greatly enhance their own skills, since the best way to learn is to teach…and rural communities would be developing local, sustainable agricultural practices.

"Wonderful!" interjected the Dean. "That's a great idea."

Christian nodded, adding, "This is not a new concept for my countrymen. In fact, each of us is well aware of the ancient 'head man's' mantra: 'Teach them how to fish…don't just give them a fish.'"

Ian then asked Dana to describe her role in the Mozambique training project.

Dana looked the administrators in the eye and began, "In addition to identifying local teacher/farmers, the attaché and I will meet with several existing co-ops in the area as well as those who market agricultural commodities. We plan to float the idea of contract farming as a way to boost the local economy. As you may be aware, at the present time virtually all cotton and tobacco produced in Mozambique is sold via contact arrangement."

A surprised look crossed the faces of the two visitors who glanced at each other. How in the world could a person so young be able to connect and partner with an official attaché?

Dana smiled and calmly said, "I suppose you're wondering about my background and how it's prepared me for such an assignment. I can certainly understand your skepticism. I actually had an opportunity to do an undergraduate internship with an Ag Attaché while he was an Extension Specialist at Iowa State. Last summer, I was able to reconnect with that attaché while working for my State Congressional Representative in Washington. You probably know that Representative Holmes is the Chairperson of the House Committee on Rural Development in Africa."

Ian added, "Dana is also familiar with contract faming, because she worked several summers as a clerk at the co-op near her home. She helped many a soy bean farmer and corn producer complete the copious amounts of annual paperwork required to participate."

"That's so true," Dana laughed, "I could tell you some stories…talk about 'teaching a man to fish…'"

The administrators relaxed, chuckled and looked convinced. They asked Kevin, Jay, Dana and Christian a number of questions about the educational plan and the situation on the ground in Mozambique: the condition of the land, the farmers who worked the land and other considerations of launching such a project.

Wagner then asked Ian to report on his research. Ian used his Power Point to update the Dean and Director on the progress of his genetics research on Jatropha. Most of this was review for them, since Ian made quarterly reports on his work – highlighting both breakthroughs and challenges. They did have a few clarification questions about his work, though, and praised the thoroughness of his reports.

The Department Chair asked if there were further questions about either of the projects that were already underway. Hearing none, he moved on to the final item on the agenda – modifications on the Energy Department's initial plan and subsequent adjustments that needed to be made by MSU. He, once again, turned the floor over to Ian.

Ian began explaining what was currently happening in Africa, "The President of Mozambique has recently changed his priorities for improving agricultural productivity in his nation. He's determined to earn a greater share of global agriculture trade, since recently, nine of ten major exports from Africa have been losing significant market share. The previous national zeal to produce more and better Jatropha oil seeds has therefore diminished and become a lower priority for him and his agricultural leaders."

"So, what does that mean for your research and your scheduled trip to Mozambique, Professor?" Experiment Station Director Schwartz asked.

Ian replied confidently, "I believe that I should stay here and focus on the genetic work we've been pursuing. We are learning more with each pilot and believe that we are getting close to solving the major issues that have prevented Jatropha from being viable in the past. "

Harry Wagner signaled his agreement and added that since Christian's assistantship was totally funded by the grant — nothing coming from USAID — he'd also be remaining on campus, something of a loss because of his ease in working with African producers and his proficiency in both Portuguese and Swahili.

Dean Wilson spoke up, "This is one of our college's major initiatives with a lot of federal dollars attached. I'm not willing to abandon or even diminish the project, just yet…I think it's important for Mr. Rosario, here, to accompany the group going to Mozambique. His background and skills are far too valuable to be left behind in East Lansing."

Pausng a moment, he then went on, "My office has some discretionary funds remaining in this year's budget. I believe we'll be able to cover Christian's stipend for a month and take care of his expenses in Africa, as well. I'll call the budget office this afternoon and take care of that."

Relief and pleasure was evident on the young man's face. Wagner was quick to voice his personal appreciation as well as that of others in the department who would be affected. He then turned to Ian to discuss possible changes to the project and new directions for the future.

Ian braced himself. "Sir," he said addressing Director Schwartz, "we would like to officially request that Dr. Taylor's appointment be adjusted to allow her to take an active part in the Jatropha project. David Mason is due to complete his doctorate shortly and begin looking for fulltime employment. His expertise and diligence will leave a big void in our laboratory operations. We'd like to have Jordan's knowledge and experience available to us as soon as possible…even as soon as the first of February, if possible."

"Dr. Taylor, what do you have to say about the request?" inquired Schwartz, her principal funder. "What's the status of your work on the ornamental weed? Will that work suffer if you have less time to spend on it?"

Jordan responded that she had hoped to become involved in Prof. Mahoney's project. She explained that she had worked with him at A & M before coming to MSU. She knew she could contribute to the project as well as learn from her former professor.

"Besides," she said earnestly, "it could well be that grasses and weeds are closer cousins than we previously thought."

Then, turning to the other part of the question, she reported, "We'll begin field trials on our ornamental grasses this spring. I've signed agreements with two landscape growers for five-year trials. We've agreed to work with them for the five years, as long as we continue to make progress. We will nullify the agreement if we are able to confirm we have a "freezing" solution or we abandon the initiative for some unforeseen reason. I would be comfortable using some of my research portfolio for the Jatropha project, especially since there could be connections between the projects. I would like to maintain the 20% teaching component of my contract, though."

The Director didn't hesitate, having more than a little knowledge about the weed investigation. "I don't see why this shift would be detrimental to your work at this time. I suspect that you've already secured your department chair's approval. She and I have discussed the need for her faculty to become more involved in inter-departmental research projects. We can always review options next fiscal year, if the trials indicate significant breakthroughs."

Jordan said that yes, she had discussed a change in her appointment with her Chair and had received her tentative approval.

Webster thanked the Director Schwartz for his flexibility. Finally, before concluding the meeting he inquired if Ian had anything more to share.

"Only one more thing," Ian said, energized by the positive responses so far, "I've learned recently about some positive research developments on Jatropha in Nigeria, Zimbabwe and Egypt. What really excites me, however, is the research of a new Japanese investigator. I've had a bit of trouble tracking down some of the missing data I need, however." He briefly described his father, Michael Mahoney's, neighbors and their possible connection to the Japanese researcher. He explained that his father had agreed to act as a liaison with the neighbors to try and locate the data that Ian needed. He confirmed that the neighbors were, indeed, delighted to help find out what they could.

The Dean laughed. "That old 'son of a gun' must have had enough time on the golf course and now wants to remove the rust from his brain cells. You know how it is with retired professors; they're just like old jockeys…itchy to get back in the saddle without the stress of competing at the Derby."

Chuckling, Ian agreed that was, most definitely, the case.

Schwartz offered one more piece of pertinent information. Unbeknownst to the others, except for Dean Wilson, a Japanese professor would be joining the Bio-Chemistry Department before the end of the semester and was looking for a way to become engaged with others in the campus research community. Jordan offered to touch base with him when he arrived, since Bio-Chem had been part of her graduate curriculum.

With no further questions or comments, the meeting was adjourned. After hand-shakes all around, Dr. Wagner escorted the two guests from the conference room and building. Cheers went up once the trio was out of earshot.

"We did it!"

"They both agreed to our requests and even had a few helpful suggestions!"

"We're all winners this morning!"

"Let's go to lunch on Ian's dime!"

And that's just what they did.

Ian was breathless that evening when he told his wife all about the successful meeting – including the demise of every single scone in the basket she had provided. In the middle of his long-detailed monologue, he smacked the side of his head with an open hand.

He just remembered that no one had mentioned that Dana was scheduled to meet with the Ag Attaché very soon. They were planning to meet at the site of a small, regionally-funded, biofuel processing plant that relied on locally-produced Jatropha seeds. The fuel produced at the plant was being used to power local buses and trucks. This could be a model for other regions in the country. What an oversight…they certainly should have mentioned it! No matter. It was precisely because Dana's funding was secure, that they hadn't thought to mention the upcoming meeting. It might be worth a follow-up memo, though, he suggested.

His wife looked amused as she leaned over to give her husband a kiss. "I'm very proud of you, you know…and you should be thrilled with your success today…not only for yourself, but for your staff, also! Of course, sometimes," she looked at him mischievously, "people forget little things like Dana's meeting!!!! — even the Phi Beta Kappa son of Mike and Kate Mahoney forgets things sometimes!"

"Leave it to you," he admitted, "to remind me that I'm only HUMAN!"

She smiled.

"Come on then, my long-suffering wife," he said, pulling her up from the couch and putting his arm around her shoulders. "Let's go to bed."

CHAPTER SEVENTEEN

That winter was full of chilly fun for the twins. Mike and Mia never seemed to tire of their many trips downhill on the sled and saucer, leaving their imprints as snow angels all over the yard and creating entire villages of snow people. When their cheeks were rosy and their mittens frozen, they rushed inside, shed their snow pants and headed downstairs. Their dad, with an assist from the handyman next door, Rod Lane, had installed the new basketball hoop with its stand in the basement. There was also space down there for them to practice their Tai Chi routines. They dribbled around the tile floor and launched shots that bounced jauntily off the rim and backboard. On those occasions when the ball actually swished through the hoop, there were enthusiastic claps and cheers.

Because of their new interest in basketball, they were getting very excited about the upcoming woman's game at the Breslin Center. For the second year in a row, they would be joining other Montessori families for the game and a pizza supper afterwards. Only five more days to mark off on the kitchen calendar where they had faithfully been keeping track.

"The game was so much fun last year," remembered Michael.

"But the best part was when Daddy came home from Africa and got to go with us and Miss Peggy to the game," Mia added.

"Miss Peggy?" quipped Michael. "Don't you mean 'Mommy?'"

"Well, she wasn't Mommy, then, Silly...but it was fun to have both Daddy and Miss Peggy with us, cheering for the Spartans," Mia remembered.

"Yeah, but this year we get to go as a FAMILY!" Mike said cheerfully.

When the four of them sat down for dinner that evening, Ian posed a question. "I've been thinking about the basketball game this weekend. Do you think we should invite Jordan to come with us? After all, she was a college basketball player, herself."

"That's a great idea," Peggy agreed enthusiastically. "We might also want to include Mrs. Webb. She's a kicky gal... and it was fun to get to know her at Thanksgiving. She might really enjoy a basketball game."

"Yeah, Daddy," Mia added, "it would be fun to have a real basketball player with us at the game. We could tell all our friends about her. Please ask her."

Ian laughed, "What do you think, Mikey? Should we include a couple of others for the game?"

Michael gave his dad a thumbs up. "Sure, Dad, maybe Jordan can tell me how to dunk!"

Peg began clearing the table, "Why don't you call Jordan right now and extend our invitation to both of them? I know the special tickets are still available. It'll be our treat."

"Well, I guess it's decided then," Ian said, pulling his smart phone from his pocket. Ian made the call and was pleased to tell the others that Jordan had accepted immediately. She had also said that she thought it would be fine with Martha, too, since they had already planned to go to the bookstore for lunch on Sunday. They could always head to the bookstore another time.

"I'm glad that nice Miss Jordan can come," said Mike, "I think she likes us."

Mia smiled and said, "Mrs. Webb was nice to us at Thanksgiving, too. I'll bet she wishes she had some grandkids around. Since Mimi, G-ma, and our Papas can't be with us, we could pretend she's part of our family."

"I think she'd like that," her mother agreed.

That Sunday, after a quick lunch following church, the quartet changed into their Spartan garb and headed to the fieldhouse. Some of their school friends along with their parents and a few grandparents were already seated, watching both teams warm up.

Jordan and her neighbor soon joined the Mahoney's. The kids were excited to see that they both wore Spartan shirts, too.

After greeting the Mahoneys and settling in her seat, Jordan admitted to Peggy, "I'm sad to say, I've not seen the women's team play yet. I have been following them in the paper, of course. Earlier this season they beat a ranked Big Ten team. Since then, however, they've been plagued with injuries and illness, so they've not played that well recently. I've only seen the Maryland gals play on tv, since they weren't in our league when I was playing at Purdue."

Martha was not a regular at the women's games either, although many of her co-workers at the Wharton gift shop were season ticket holders and had urged her to join them. Seats for the women's games were inexpensive and easily available. The games were always well-attended. Today, excitement for the game was building as Sparty, the cheerleaders and the pep band got the crowd involved.

Peg noticed that Paul and a young woman she did not

recognize had joined the Montessori group. Peg wondered who she was — perhaps someone Paul had started to date?

It was time for the game to begin. Jordan was pleased to see that one of the officials was a woman. She immediately commented to her friends, "See how tall that visiting center is? No wonder they've been able to beat Ohio State twice this season. Usually, the Buckeye women have tall centers; at least that's how I remember them. As you might guess, I hated to play the Buckeyes…especially at their place."

"Why does that girl dribble so much? Why doesn't she just shoot the ball?" Mia wanted to know.

"Honey, that's because the other team is playing really good defense. It's hard for her to pass the ball to her teammate who's probably a better shooter then she is. That gal is called the point guard. It's her job to pass the ball to other girls who have good shots. She's only supposed to shoot herself, if she's pretty sure she can make the basket," was the former player's analysis.

The kids watched the game, talked to their friends, cheered with the cheerleaders and the time passed quickly. "Wow!" Mike said as the buzzer went off and the women sat down on the bench. "It's halftime already?"

Jordan explained to the boy that it was only the end of the first quarter. She told him that the women's rules had recently changed; and that unlike men's basketball, which still had two halves, women's basketball now played four quarters, instead. She said that it means they get more breaks than the men, even though they play the same number of total minutes.

"There's another change, since I played basketball in high school," offered Mrs. Webb. "Back in the old days, we played with a six-person team. Nobody could cross the center line, so only the forwards could shoot and score. The guards' role was to defend."

"Wow," said Michael, wide-eyed, "you played basketball?"

Martha laughed out loud. "Yup, I sure did, Young Man, and I was a dead-eye shooter, too."

He looked at her with unabashed wonder and admiration, "Wow," he said, again.

His parents looked at each other and chuckled. Everyone continued to watch the game and Sparty's antics on the sideline. At intermission, the usher who had shown them to their seats presented each family with a large colorful poster of the Spartan team. Jordan was quick to give the one she received to Ian so each of the children could have one. Martha, playing the typical grandmother role, came down the steps carrying two large bags of popcorn and bottles of water for Jordan and the Mahoney's. Everyone in their section cheered when the school's name appeared on the large overhead screen as the day's special guests.

Play resumed as the group munched away on the popcorn. The score was close. Neither team was able to get more than a few points ahead. The lead went back and forth in the closing minutes of the game.

"The women seem to have a lot of turnovers," commented Ian.

"True enough," explained the group's expert. "They really like to run and shoot, which leads to frequent missed passes and shots taken too quickly...but it sure keeps the game moving. I think the fast pace makes it even more exciting for fans."

"Go Green! Go White!" Mia screamed with the rest of the crowd, clapping loudly. Everyone was standing and urging the girls to shoot. Unfortunately, in the final seconds of the game, a player in red threw up a longshot and made a three-point basket. Game over. A blanket of silence fell over the crowd. Another disappointing loss for the green and white.

After a few comments about how well the Spartans played and how lucky that last basket was, the group gathered their things and headed off for the promised pizza. The Montessori Community found their seats in one of the back rooms of the pizza place. There was a lot of chatter as benches at the long tables filled. The Mahoney group found places with Jodie, Ben and B.J., along with one of Mia's friends and her folks. As the wait staff began to take orders, Paul and his date arrived, too late to join the already-filled table.

"Hi there, My Friends," was his greeting, "I'd like you to meet my guest, Tammy Sue Randolph. She, too, is relatively new to Michigan. Tammy Sue, these are the folks I was telling you about…Ian and Peggy Mahoney and their twins, Mike and Mia. These are the Allens: Jodie, Dr. Ben and B.J. And this," he said turning to the others in the group, "is Martha Webb and her neighbor, Jordan Taylor. Both Ian and Jordan are professors at State. "

"I'm so pleased to meet y'all," responded the pretty young woman with an obvious southern drawl. "Paul told me all about your wonderful Thanksgivin' Celebration. I hope we'll see you around." Off they went to find vacant seats in another part of the room.

After a brief nod, the children went back to their conversations with their friends. The looks that were exchanged among the adults told quite a different story, however. The Allens looked confused, the Mahoneys were surprised and Mrs. Webb looked concerned when she noticed the look of dismay and surprise on Jordan's face. The others at the table had missed the whole episode, since they had left the table to speak with other friends.

After the meal, the green and white fans went home —

stomachs filled, still feeling disappointed about the loss. Later that night, after story and prayers, the twins were happy to turn in for the night — for a change. Their parents were equally tired but sat up in bed for a few minutes to reflect on the recent encounter between Paul and Jordan.

"It was nice that so many families were able to participate," Peg said first. "They give us a real deal on the tickets, practically giveaways for groups like ours. That way, even many of the scholarship youngsters are able to enjoy the game, although some skipped the pizza party, I noticed. I hope we can change that, if we do a repeat next year."

"I didn't realize that the tickets were discounted. What a smart PR move on their part. It's never too soon to attract new and young fans," observed the come-lately-himself fan."

The conversation then shifted to what had really been on both of their minds — Paul's young companion. Should they think of her as his "lady friend?" "Girlfriend" certainly didn't seem appropriate at their ages...and it was only a basketball game, after all. Perhaps they weren't even officially dating.

Trying to focus on the right term for Paul's friend was impossible. In the end they decided that Paul probably was seeing Tammy Sue socially. They figured that she was the one who worked for Community Education and was feeding him information about home-schooled candidates for his basketball league.

"What did you think of Tammy Sue?" Peg wanted to know.

"She's quite attractive, very friendly and certainly southern. Since he's from Virginia, that might be an easy connection," Ian suggested.

After thinking a minute, his wife confirmed that she was probably the person from the Singles Can group that Paul had mentioned. Seeing who was in the congregation on Sunday mornings was not easy for choir members, so she hadn't seen her at church.

"Tammy Sue would certainly be hard to miss, especially by the men in attendance," quipped Peg. "Did you see Jordan's face when he introduced them? She looked...I don't know...surprised for sure...maybe perturbed. Do you think she might have some second thoughts about her negative reactions to Paul's initial attempts to get to know her."

Peg guessed that Paul had probably decided that his efforts to interest Jordan in joining the church group was a lost cause. She clearly had issues with religion for some reason. Peg suggested that Paul appeared to have already forgotten about Jordan and moved on. Why not, with the seemingly available and attractive Ms. Randolph nearby?

"I don't know," interjected Ian, "Paul seems like the kind of guy who likes a challenge. He doesn't seem to be the type who gives up easily. While he and Tammy Sue may have common religious and southern backgrounds, she sort of seemed out of place at a basketball game. Look how she was dressed for a sporting event and did you see how she seemed to be talking throughout the game...ignoring the action on the court? Jordan and he, on the other hand, share a love for hoops...and he certainly seemed interested in her when we first introduced them. Look at us...it took a little while to find out what we had in common...but interests and values are so important in a relationship."

As the former Ms. Gerber reflected on Ian's comment, she couldn't help mentally listing their many differences. He was a professor, the only son of professional, well-traveled parents. She, on the other hand, was a farm girl from rural Michigan – someone who made her own clothes, had limited travels, came from a big family and spent her days with children in a preschool. Yet, somehow, they had let love happen.

As if reading her thoughts, Ian countered with, "Peg, it's pretty amazing to me how much you and I had in common, even though we didn't recognize it at first. I liked you and your parents from the beginning, and being in agriculture at the university, I have to admit, I was jealous of your farm background. Your dad's perspective is always enlightening to me. He's a successful agri-businessman who keeps up with all the newest trends. Our conversations are always thought-provoking. He and my dad have agriculture in common, as well…and their values and zest for church and community involvement is so alike. Your mother and mine could be sisters, they've become that close. And you…you have a mind that is open for anything. You are so capable and practical. You are fun and see the beauty in everything around you. It was my lucky day when you agreed to spend time with me."

Laughing, Peg responded, "Wait a minute, Dr. Mahoney, wasn't it I who asked you to join the high school youth group to fix that porch last year? I don't think it was you who pursued me!"

"Well, okay then…it was my lucky day when you allowed me to join you with those crazy teenagers. You have taught me more about life and love than you will ever know," he said, pulling her close and kissing her gently.

"How fortunate for me that you think so," she said returning his kiss, "but I think we taught each other about those things. And I agree that our parents' friendship is amazing! But…back to the point…what, if anything, did you read into Jordan's reaction to seeing Paul with another woman?"

"Hard to say," Ian hesitated. "The two women appear to be totally different. We know Jordan and Paul share a love of basketball, but after that…who knows. I'm not as perceptive to the nuances of emotions as you are. I guess we'll just have to wait and see. Only the Lord knows what's in store for any of his children."

With that, the couple turned off the light, nestled together…each with his/her own thoughts about Paul, Tammy Sue, Jordan and their own amazing journey. The house on Ottawa Drive became silent as the residents settled in for the night.

CHAPTER EIGHTEEN

As Martha finished cleaning up after her supper, she wondered if her young friend would be spending another long night at the office. She hadn't seen Jordan all week. This was obviously a busy time for the professor, since she was having to adjust her schedule to accommodate the new on-campus assignment, while still making trips to her field trial sites.

Martha had been quite busy herself. Last week, she attended a benefit tea at the Okemos Interfaith Chapel. The tea featured a display of quilts made by a group of church women. They were being sold to raise funds to send to the Chapel's partner church in Mozambique. That church would be using the money to purchase children's books for their local school.

She had also been helping Rod Lane at several of his recent book signings. Today's signing event had been at the Ojibwa Montessori School. What fun that had been. The children asked so many interesting questions. One child she thought was young Michael Mahoney raised a rather strange question, "Mr. Rod, are Indians the only ones who have tribal council meetings?"

"Good question, Son," Rod had replied. "Only the Indians call them tribal councils, but lots of other folks have meetings when they need to solve problems. Sometimes they even call those groups of people 'councils.' I wouldn't be surprised if you've had such meetings at your own house."

Just then there was a knock on the door that separated her apartment from the house next door.

"Hello there, Neighbor," called out Jordan. "Long time, no see. Here are those books I've been telling you about." Jordan handed over a stack of three or four books. "I've been so busy with the trials and shifting gears on campus that I forgot all about sharing the books with you. Sorry to be so absent-minded."

"No problem, My Dear," Martha responded, taking the books and putting them on a side table. "I've been busy too…especially helping with book signings for Rod Lane. I've been worried about you, though. If you could, I'll bet you would even sleep at your office. You're certainly giving more than 100% to your duties."

"That's a thought," Jordan said. "I actually heard one of our graduate students who did an internship in Washington, say that a number of the younger members of congress do just that…sleep in their offices. For them, though, it's really more about saving money than actually working long hours."

"So, do you have anything fun on the horizon?" the older woman wanted to know.

"Funny you should mention it, Martha," Jordan said, moving further into the room and heading over to the kitchen table. "There is something I've been mulling over in my mind. Maybe talking it over with you will help me decide what to do this weekend. Are you busy right now?"

"I'm never too busy for you, My Dear. Come on in, and I'll get us some coffee," Martha said grabbing two mugs from the cupboard and filling each with steaming brew. She was pleased to be with her friend, again…and warmed by the fact that Jordan wanted her advice.

After accepting a cup of hot coffee and settling into her favorite chair, Jordan went on to explain that she had been invited to attend two events for the upcoming weekend. This year, the Final Four Men's Basketball Tournament was being held in Detroit at the new Caesar's Palace Arena. One of her Purdue roommates, Valerie Jones, was a sports writer for the "Detroit Free Press." Val wanted her to stay with her in her loft apartment downtown and attend the games. She had an extra ticket for the games, thanks to her press credentials.

"That sounds like a ball…a real basketBALL!" Martha laughed, heartily. "What a great opportunity to reconnect with a friend and see some great basketball at the same time. It'd be a nice break for you, too!"

"Oh, Martha, I've always wanted to go to a Final Four, but it just hasn't been in the cards," Jordan admitted. "This year's tourney is really something special…both Purdue and Indiana University are playing in it!"

"Who will they be playing…are Duke or Kentucky in the Final Four? Seems like they usually are," Martha said, surprising her friend, once again.

"And you claim to know little about b-ball. Shame on you, Grandmother Webb, for not admitting that you follow sports," Jordan admonished her good-naturedly, before continuing. "This year, yes, it will be Duke, again, and also North Carolina. They, like Kentucky and Kansas, seem to have luck wearing blue team uniforms. So, it will be Big 10 versus ACC…and it should be very exciting. It's just that I have so much to do. I should be in the office this weekend. I mean, I could just watch the games on the tv in the office break room, then get back to work. But…"

Jordan went on to tell Martha all about the big weekend activities. She explained that since this year it would actually be two Indiana teams versus two from North Carolina, the governors of the two states decided to hold rival state galas in adjoining ballrooms of the arena on Friday night. As a former Boilermaker player, Valerie had received an invitation for the Friday night party. There would be food, appearances by former coaches, music all night long and even a pep rally.

"That sounds amazing! Now you listen to me, Miss Jordan," Martha said sternly, straightening to her full (though limited) height in her chair and looking Jordan directly in the eye. "You need a break, My Child. Trust me, if you don't take time for yourself, your work will begin to suffer. I know we always think that working harder is better, but to be successful…you need to work smarter. In this case, 'smarter' means to work hard until Friday…then head to Detroit for the weekend…so that you will be mentally refreshed and ready to work long hours again next week. The last thing you want to do is burn out! So, it's decided…you will go and really enjoy yourself. Besides, it sounds like quite a bash."

Jordan leaned over and hugged her surrogate grandmother. "Martha, you are really something. How could I even begin to argue with you? I guess that's why I came over here…I needed someone to give me permission to do something for myself. And, of course, I know you're right about burning out. I've seen others do it…I've just been trying so hard to be successful on all fronts."

"I know, Dear," Martha said, patting her hand. "That's why you're so good at what you do. You care. You're committed. And now you're going to have some fun!"

But, Martha," Jordan said, after a pause, "I just realized, I don't have anything to wear to a gala. My wardrobe these days is pretty limited to duds for gardening and what they call 'business casual.'"

But Martha was not to be deterred. She went to her desk

and pulled out a coupon she'd received in yesterday's mail.

"Here, Young Lady, use this coupon for Chico's big sale. You probably got one yesterday too. I've never been there, but I've heard others say it's a store that carries a lot of kicky clothes that would be perfect for Friday night's event. And if you can't find anything there, you can always head over to the mall to find something. You need to part with some of that hard-earned cash…and splurge on yourself! You also need to pick up a Purdue t-shirt or two…then you'll be set for the weekend."

Jordan looked at her neighbor and grinned. Martha Webb may be 80, but she's certainly young-at-heart. There are no "buts" about it, decided Dr. Taylor.

"OK, Grandmother Webb…far be it for me to question your sage advice," Jordan stated emphatically. "I'm going to do it. Detroit here I come." As she put her mug on the counter and turned to go, she hugged her friend one more time. Then she was off to check her stack of unopened mail. Two coupons would be better than one. She would start at Chico's and see if they had anything that would be appropriate. After all, it would be fun to have something with glitz and shimmer in her closet for a change. She couldn't remember the last time she bought…or wore…something like that!

Little did the Boilermaker know that Paul Franklin was heading to the Final Four, as well. In his case, former Bergamo Hawks teammate Rick Marks, who was now an Assistant coach at IU, had called him and asked if he wanted to come join him for the weekend. They had not seen each other, since returning from Europe. Rick knew Paul was in the Lansing area, so thought it might be easy for him to come down. He had both game tickets and tickets to the Governors' Gala. He would also have two beds in his hotel room where the IU players were staying, so Paul was welcome to crash there. He reminded Paul that, of course, he'd be expected to wear red and white and cheer the Hoosiers on to another national title.

Paul, like all college basketball enthusiasts, loved the Final Four. What an opportunity, he thought. He'd pick up a couple of IU t-shirts and pack something for the gala (Didn't he have a red and white striped tie somewhere?). It sounded like a fun weekend. Of course, he loved the Final Four. He would be glued to the tube, if he were at home, so he might as well drive down and watch in person. Besides, he and Rick had become good friends while playing in Europe, and it would be great to see him again.

On Friday morning, Jordan went next door to model for Martha what she'd purchased at Chico's. As she stepped into Martha's apartment, Martha gasped. Jordan stood there in her dressy black chiffon pants that flowed over her long, shapely legs. Her glittering gold tunic fit her perfectly and the neckline plunged to accentuate her stunning figure. Martha could not believe her eyes. Jordan was always dressed in baggy casual or professional-looking work clothes. She had never seen her look so fetching and…well…sexy. Martha couldn't speak at first, so she just gave her friend a two-thumbs up.

Then she smiled in wonderment. "Wow," she gushed, "Who would have known that such an amazing butterfly has been hidden in that cocoon of yours all this time?" She looked at Jordan for a minute, then disappeared into her bedroom. She returned with a small black purse and a black velvet bag. "I bet you never thought about accessories. I'd like to loan you this small purse and these flashy black pearl earrings and bracelet, if you think they'd work."

Jordan blushed, "You're right again, oh, Wise One, I never gave such things a thought. They are perfect! I promise I'll take good care of them. You know, I always wear these same silver-stud earrings, since they seem to go with everything, and I just forget to change them. I don't have anything with bling. I will wear them, for sure…that way, you can be there in absentia with me! Thank you, so much!"

Jordan turned to go, then paused and turned back, looking sheepish as she continued, "I do have a little confession to make, though, Martha. At Chico's, they told me that there was only one coupon per householder that could be used on sale items. Sooo, I fibbed a bit. I said that one came from my house, and the other came to my Grandmother's apartment. The clerk laughed and thought it was great that I had a granny in town who could help me out. You know what? She was right…I'm unbelievably lucky to have 'my granny' right next door!"

She hugged her friend tightly, gave a friendly wave and hurried home to finish packing. As she tucked the purse and black velvet bag into her suitcase, she couldn't help but smile…even as a tiny tear glistened in the corner of her eye. She was lucky, she thought. Actually, she was blessed (if one believed in such things) to have such an amazing woman in her life. She threw her bag into the car and headed east for what promised to be an awesome weekend in the Motor City.

CHAPTER NINETEEN

Jordan had a leisurely trip to Detroit on Friday afternoon. It was good to reconnect with her Purdue roommate. Valerie had gone on to get a graduate degree in journalism at the University of Missouri and then had had several writing gigs on weekly publications before landing her position at the Free Press. Her loft apartment was in an old factory building and had a lot of character. Val had an apartment mate, but she was out of town, hence the vacant bed for Jordan. They had a pleasant visit before the journalist had to leave to conduct interviews prior to that evening's event. The plan was for her to visit with retired coaches from both IU and Purdue before they were mobbed by party-goers.

Jordan had fun getting ready for the gala. She applied her makeup carefully and opted for a sweeping up-do that accentuated her neck...and neckline. Once she arrived, Jordan hoped to find a small table in an obscure corner where she could privately munch on the fine array of finger foods and enjoy her usual crowd-watching until Valerie was able to join her.

Although many of the party-goers were chatting excitedly as they gravitated from group to group, and the two bands were alternating sets; the decibel level was not as high as Jordan might have expected. Luck was with her. She filled her plate, grabbed a Diet Coke and found an out-of-the-way table near a doorway.

Just as she got settled, someone suddenly approached her table from around the corner. It was a tall fellow wearing a sport coat, white shirt and a bright red and white striped tie. He stopped short, when he saw her...not recognizing her at first.

"Uh...Jordan?...Jordan Taylor? I can't believe I just ran into the famous Dr. Jordan Taylor...here! What...what in the world are you doing here?" Paul stammered.

Paul was completely flummoxed. He was surprised to see her, of course, but even more surprised to see her looking so dazzling. He reddened, then shook his head apologetically and resumed, "I mean...sorry...of course, you're here for the games...your homeboys are playing in the Final Four. I just didn't expect to see anyone I knew... But of course, you actually played for Purdue, so this will be a big weekend for you."

Paul's discomfort gave Jordan a couple of minutes to corral her own surprise at seeing Paul, but not her unexpected feelings of pleasure at his embarrassment...and his presence. She couldn't help but smile inwardly.

"Well, this is a surprise," she said, standing and working hard to keep her voice friendly and casual. What brings you here, Mr. Franklin? I didn't know you were an IU fan. Nice tie! Always good to wear the right school colors."

Paul could not keep his eyes off Jordan, although he struggled to focus on her face, only. "Well, I've never been an IU fan, per se, and although I was too young to remember, I certainly heard about the Hoosiers Final Four successes under Bobby Knight...and I really wanted Tom Crean to be successful there. I wonder if they'll be here. By the way, if you don't mind my mentioning it, you look fabulous in your black and gold outfit."

Jordan blushed, suddenly felt self-conscious, but she didn't respond to his remark. Instead, she said, "I know Coach Knight as well as Coach Keady are here; because my college roommate, Valerie Jones, is supposed to interview them both. She's a sports reporter for the 'Free Press' and is hosting me this weekend. I assume you're going to the games. How did you happen to snag tickets?"

"Valerie Jones was your roommate at Purdue? Wow! I follow her in the 'Free Press'…she's really quite good. I'd love to meet her," Paul said admiringly. "Actually, the last time… no, the only other time…I got to go to a Final Four was when I was in fifth grade. My dad took me to the championship weekend in Atlanta. This time, I'm here thanks to one of my former Hawk teammates, Rick Marks, who's now an IU Assistant Coach. I'm sharing his room at the team hotel. Needless to say, he's pretty busy, so I haven't seen too much of him. He had extra tickets, though…so here I am."

"So, you're at the gala by yourself, then?" she asked.

"Yup, just me, I'm afraid. This is really quite the party, though. When will Valerie be joining you?" Paul wanted to know.

"She wasn't sure," Jordan went on to explain. "She hoped to catch Knight and Keady, as I said, but she also needs to try to get scoops on game plans, injury status, starting lineups, etc., with assistants, players or anyone else she sees. There are no formal press conferences scheduled tonight, so it'll all depends on who she is able to corral for a chat. Several coaches and players will be here attending the pep rally later, so I hope I'll see her at some point. If not, we'll meet back at the room after the gala."

Jordan decided it wouldn't kill her to invite Paul to share her table. How bad could it be? They'd both be eating and listening to the music, so there'd be no need to carry on a deep conversation. Besides, Paul would be better than having some strange guy invade her space and even put the make on her. Franklin knew better than to waste his time on her... and, after all, he was dating Miss Southern Belle Tammy Sue, back in East Lansing.

"Why don't you get a plate and sit down," Jordan offered lightly. "There don't seem to be many empty tables now... and I'm sure Val will be here soon."

"Thanks, Jordan, I will," he said, relieved that she did not order him away, like she'd dismissed him at the Mahoneys'. "I'll grab a plate and be right back. Can I get you anything?"

"No, thanks, I'm fine," Jordan began, then added, "Well, maybe one of those cupcakes, if you can. Thanks."

So, the two sat enjoying the food and music. Both acted like gawking teenagers, as they strained to see famous coaches and players, sports' announcers and celebrity fans. Jordan and Paul chatted comfortably about their favorite teams, past March Madness upsets and basketball in general. They even got to see Coaches Knight and Keady, when the band leader handed them the mike for a few comments during a break. When the pep bands led cheers, they laughingly joined in both rallies that ended with the singing of their school fight songs.

As people began filing out of the ballroom, Jordan looked around for Valerie. She stood up and grabbed her coat and purse. "Well, I'm guessing Val had a successful evening. She just texted that she'd meet me at home. What a great idea it was to have a gala tonight," Jordan said. "I'm so glad I decided to come. I'm just sorry we didn't get to hook up with Val. I know she's on deadline, though, so I'm sure she'll be finishing her column back at the apartment. I think she said it had to be in by eleven."

"I had a great time, too," agreed Paul, "and thanks for letting me join you. It was nice to be able to talk 'hoops' with someone who really knows and appreciates the game. I'm sorry I didn't get to meet Valerie...but perhaps later this weekend. So, where's Val's place? Do you need a cab? The Hilton is only about two blocks away."

"Oh, I know where the Hilton is. My place is even closer than that but on the other side of the street."

Paul donned his coat, then bowed dramatically, "Dr. Taylor, my mother always said, 'never let a lady walk home alone'...so Ma'am, may I have the pleasure of walking you home?"

"Franklin," she laughed, "you're one of a kind! I can't decide if you're a true southern gentleman or a comedian in disguise. Sir, in either case, I accept. Let's go."

They each grabbed a bottle of water from a tub by the door and began their walk home. Because they sensed immediately that they were both power-walkers, their pace was fast and conversation impossible. When they arrived at their destination, both were a bit winded, so they plopped down on a bench in front of her residence to catch their breaths.

"I don't know about you, Doc, but I'm more out of shape than I thought...and you were chugging along in those heels, too!" Paul said, gasping a little.

"Me too," she laughed between pants, "and my poor feet are complaining, I have to admit. Or maybe we're just older than we'd like to think. By the way, there's a question I've been wanting to ask someone; and since you're handy, here it goes...do you know anything about a 'Stop and Go' Detroit Tour? I was hoping to do it with Valerie on Sunday, but she'll be in press conferences all afternoon."

"That's interesting...I read about that tour, myself. In fact, I was going to invite Rick to join me for the special five-hour version on Sunday afternoon, but he'll be tied up with the team all day…win or lose. That tour's the sort of thing that's more fun, if you have a buddy."

"My name's not 'Buddy,' but maybe we could pretend it is and take the tour together. Do you know where we sign up?" She couldn't believe she was suggesting they actually spend the afternoon together. Oh, well – why not?

"There's a kiosk in my hotel lobby where I can sign us both up as soon as I get back," Paul offered.

"That would be great, Paul," she said, relieved, then added, "You'll need my credit card, of course."

"Your credit's good, Professor, remember, I know where you live," he laughed. "We can take care of the finances on Sunday. The tour starts at 1:00 and will pick us up at my hotel. It ends after an early dinner stop in Greek Town. Be sure to get to the Hilton early, so we can get good seats on the bus. I'm planning to go to the Mariners' Chapel for the early service Sunday morning. Do you want to join me? The chapel's really quite historic," he asked with a wink.

"Don't press your luck, Buddy," Jordan responded with mock indignation. "Thanks for walking me home, Paul. Your Mother would be proud of you."

"The pleasure was all mine," Paul responded, then said soberly, "Maybe you'll think this is a little corny, Jordan, but sometimes I feel my mom's presence…as if she's smiling down on me. I call her my 'Guardian Angel.'"

Jordan looked at Paul with surprise and slowly nodded. Then she said, quietly, "No, Paul, I don't think that's silly at all. I sometimes feel that same way about my dad, though I call him my 'Knight in Shining Armor' not my 'Guardian Angel.'"

And so, they parted. Each wondered why he and she had felt so comfortable in the other's presence for a change. Maybe they could develop a friendship, after all. Well, they'd just have to see how the weekend unfolded.

CHAPTER TWENTY

It had been several years since Jordan had attended a men's basketball game, so being at the preliminary round of a Final Four was special. Her seat was in a great spot behind the Purdue bench. Up close, the players looked so tall! Both teams, she observed, had at least one seven-footer. She couldn't believe that every seat in the enormous facility was filled. There were lots of children there, and many people in wheel chairs. We really are making amazing progress in ensuring facilities are handicap-accessible, she thought.

The game was off to a slow start – too many off-balance three-pointers, especially on the part of North Carolina. The Boilermakers were playing tough defense, which reminded her of her own Boilermaker team so many years ago. Big Ten teams have always been recognized for their consistently tough defense, she remembered.

An older man sitting next to her made continual remarks throughout the first half, "Why don't we shoot more? That guard traveled! Call it! Are you kidding me? You gotta drive to the basket more! Great shot! Wow…did you see that alley-oop?" Turning to Jordan he said urgently, "Hey, come on, Missy. Stand up and cheer!"

Caught up in the growing excitement of the game, Jordan ended up doing just that. During intermission, she was not sorry when the talker was replaced by a teenager, who was just as excited about the game but didn't comment on every play. In the second half, the game continued to be back and forth, but as the minutes waned, the game again got tight. Then the Boilermakers launched three, long shots in a row. The Tar Heels starting creeping back, cutting the lead to four with 30 seconds remaining. Everyone was on his/her feet, cheering and screaming. After the Boilermakers made critical free throws in the last ten seconds, the game finally ended in a Purdue win! Jordan hugged the teenager and everyone else nearby. Everyone was screaming, cheering and even crying. Jordan was totally caught up in the basketball frenzy. It brought back such vivid memories of her own playing career. She suddenly realized how much she had missed this. The Boilermakers were off to the finals on Monday night!

Jordan, and all the other fans in attendance, took a break after the game. She smiled as she watched North Carolina fans selling their tickets outside the arena to Purdue fans who had hoped to watch the finals in person. It was both loud and raucous (Purdue fans) and stunningly silent (North Carolina faithful) outside on the street. After a walk and a quick meal, Jordan returned to the arena to watch the Indiana-Duke game. While, again caught up in the excitement of the game, she found she was less nervous about the outcome, since her beloved Boilermakers had already made the finals. She hoped Indiana would pull out a victory but was not too surprised to see Duke prevail in the end. Well, at least one Big Ten team would be in the championship game. She couldn't wait until Monday!

Val and Jordan were up early on Sunday, despite a late Saturday night. After the post-game news conferences, Val had rushed back to the apartment to post her column. In the meantime, Jordan ordered takeout. Finally, an exhausted Valerie Jones plopped down on the couch next to her friend.

They dug into their bowls of pad thai (their old-time, favorite Thai dish) and alternately watched ESPN highlights and chattered on about the game, their lives and getting together again sometime soon.

"I'm so sorry we haven't had that much time together, Jordan," Val said, apologetically. "I knew I'd be busy…but this is more than even I expected. I've never done a Final Four before, so I didn't realize it would be four, fourteen-hour-plus days in a row! I feel like I've left you totally on your own!"

Jordan smiled at her friend and reassured her that she had thoroughly enjoyed the weekend so far. The gala, the game, the apartment…and even being in Detroit, again… had all been fabulous. She reminded Val that she had, after all, hooked up with Paul Franklin the night before, and they ended up having a great time. So, she was hardly alone! And besides, it was thanks to Val that she had been able to revive her passion for round ball. She admitted that she had continued to be a casual fan, since her playing days…but her passion for the game had waned after her basketball career-ending injury and the death of her father.

"I don't know how I can ever thank you for re-igniting my spark for the game, Val," Jordan said earnestly, "and for the chance to reconnect with you. I guess I didn't even realize how much I'd missed our talks. This weekend has been a real gift, Val, thank you."

The gals finished their feast, put away the remnants and wearily climbed to the loft, where they both collapsed into dream-filled sleep.

Both Val and Jordan were up early on Sunday. They shared a breakfast of bagels, bananas and coffee; then Val took off for what promised to be another long day.

Jordan took her time showering and dressing for her outing. It surprised her that she was really looking forward to an afternoon with Mr. Franklin. Her morning was leisurely...and she had time for a light lunch before heading to the Hilton.

The day was sunny, albeit a bit chilly, but still a great day to tour of a city making a comeback. She crossed the street and sat down in the lobby of the hotel, waiting for her "buddy" to join her for their outing.

"It's strange..." she thought, "I've really felt comfortable around Paul, since he's stopped treating me like a possible 'date.' He's actually easy to be around, and he has a great sense of humor. I guess I'd have to agree with what Ian said to me the other day. Despite what some people think, men and women can enjoy meaningful friendships without romance becoming an inevitable outcome."

Her thoughts were interrupted by the approach of the subject of her musing.

"Hi, Jordan," was Paul's cheery greeting. "Congratulations on Purdue's nice win yesterday. The fans around me were going wild. Too bad our game didn't turn out so well. My hotel is pretty quiet, now that many of the IU team and most of the fans are heading back to Bloomington. Rick is staying for a bunch of meetings and the championship, so I'm not going to lose my bed. Hey, the bus is here...let's go join our group."

The tour guide was very knowledgeable about the city, and her running commentary was both lively and informative. There were short stops to visit historic buildings – places like the renovated Opera House, the nearly century-old Detroit Athletic Club, churches that had been part of the Underground Railroad, the historic Guardian Building with its Art-Deco lobby, the Joe Louis Fist Sculptures, the imposing Renaissance Center, Ford Field and even the Motown Museum. There was a drive through various ethnic neighborhoods and an hour-long stop at the Detroit Institute of Arts.

Paul and Jordan especially enjoyed that stop. Paul preferred the modern art collection; Jordan liked the impressionists. They also had an on-going discussion – sometimes verging on debate – about the kind of music that was best. Neither voted for Rock or Country music, but Paul enjoyed singing Gospel songs in the choir; and he also liked classical music, since he'd been brought up with a mother who was both a piano teacher and a church organist. Jorden liked show tunes and jazz. They found they could both agree that they loved Motown music – especially after they visited the very place where the Jackson 5, Temptations and the Supremes had gotten their start.

Then it was time for the final stop in Greek Town with its many recommended eateries. "You know…Greek Town has more than moussaka and baklava…there are some great Italian restaurants, too. I vote for Italian," suggested Jordan, knowing Paul's love for eating – and cooking Italian food.

"Sounds good to me…how about real Italian pizza," was Paul's response.

"Is our pizza like what you had in Italy? It all tastes about the same to me. My taste buds are pretty midwestern, not at all gourmet. Of course, I can be really picky when it comes to eating Mexican…no Taco Bell for me," said the one-time Texan. "I read that Pizza Papalis is supposed to be one of the best in Greek Town. What do you say, Paul?"

"Well, I heard that Supino's is known for its strange toppings like eggs and turkey…who knows, they may even add some rattlesnake," Paul suggested with a sly smile. "I'm all for being creative, once in awhile. Let's go there. What do you think?"

"You have to be kidding, Paul! Rattlesnake? Yuck!" Jordan said, incredulously. "No way! Here we go…disagreeing again. Were you a debater in high school, by any chance?"

"Nope! Okay, how 'bout this?" offered the negotiator, reaching into his pocket. "Let's flip a coin to decide. Heads you win and tails I get to choose."

Before she could respond, the coin was flipped into the air. Fortunately, it was heads, so she didn't have to argue again. Off they went to Papalis, where the pizza promised to be awesome – and it was! Jordan grabbed the check and insisted on paying the bill, since Paul had refused her money for the tour tickets earlier in the day, and she certainly didn't want to be beholden to this man. Keep it simple and the finances even, was her thought.

The twosome was well-filled as they walked back toward their respective lodgings for the night. They were eager for the championship game – Purdue versus Duke. It should be a great game. On that point, for once, they agreed. Jordan had to admit, she was giddy with excitement.

Once again, Paul walked to the Hilton via Val's apartment building. Keeping the tone light, they agreed that it had been a good idea take the tour and share a pizza that day. They parted ways with a wave and a friendly, "Perhaps, we'll bump into each other at Little Caesar's tomorrow."

Jordan and Val reconnected soon after Jordan arrived at the apartment. With only one game left and fewer teams and players to follow, Val had ended her day earlier than usual. She suggested they head out for a late dessert before retiring. Jordan readily agreed, and the two had a chance to share their days' activities and predictions for tomorrow's game over a shared piece of hot molten lava cake topped with homemade vanilla ice cream. As a fellow Boilermaker, Val was as excited as Jordan for the game. They laughed and talked basketball strategy as they dug their spoons into the decadent dessert. Talk turned to Val's assignment of following college teams – especially the Boilermakers – through the NCAA tournament.

"I have to admit," she said frowning, "it's challenging to be impartial…and I work very hard not to let my readers know whom I favor in the tournament. After all, I'm working for a Detroit daily…not a local West Lafayette paper. I often have one of my co-workers peek at my work, before I submit to my editor. I'm still new enough to need a little reassurance from colleagues."

Jordan laughed, "I think that's true of us all…not only in our jobs, but in our lives." Jordan went on to tell Val about Martha Webb, and how she played just such a role for Jordan in her life.

Finally, the two headed back to the apartment and retired for the night. Neither thought they would get much sleep. They were way too excited about the upcoming game!

The next morning the two, once again, shared a quick breakfast, before preparing for the day. Val shouldered her computer bag and purse and headed for the door. The friends bid each other farewell, since they knew they would not be seeing each other again, before Jordan had to leave. Jordan expressed her heartfelt thanks, once again; and the friends exchanged hugs and promises to get together soon. Then Val was off.

Jordan donned her jeans and her second, new Purdue top, then completed her outfit with a black and gold scarf, which she had purchased on Saturday. She headed to Little Caesar's for the pep rally before the Monday night game and, of course, to again people-watch – something she never tired of doing. After the pep rally, Jordan went back to the apartment to check her email and return messages on work-related items that had arrived earlier that day. Then she headed back to the arena for the game.

But as she was waiting in line to go through the metal detector, who should come strolling by, but Paul Franklin. Much to her surprise, he, too, was wearing a Purdue sweatshirt and was carrying a bag purchased at one of the special tournament kiosks.

"Just look at you, Paul Franklin, I'm surprised to see that you've become a Boilermaker fan," Jordan teased. "So much for team loyalty! I'd say you are fickle…but you do look great in the black and gold of my alma mater!"

"Well, Miss Jordan," Paul responded, opening his coat to fully display the Boilermaker on his chest. "I always say, if you can't beat 'em…join 'em!"

"I guess that works," she laughed. "Besides, I think the black and gold suits you much better than the red and white of Indiana. What's in that bag you're carrying?" asked the always curious, but seldom nosey, Jordan.

"My dad, the former coach, gets a kick out of what my sister refers to as 'sports trinkets and trash,' so I picked up a bunch of souvenirs to commemorate this Final Four. I'll use them as stocking stuffers next Christmas." And then with a sheepish grin, he pulled out a smaller bag from his pocket and handed it to his friend.

"What's this?" Jordan asked warily.

"Well, look in the bag and see," was his rejoinder.

Cautiously opening the bag, Jordan peeked inside, then pulled out the gaudiest pair of black and gold, beaded earrings that she'd ever seen. Dangling from each of the beaded hoops was a giant Purdue 'P.'" Jordan laughed merrily. "Oh, Paul, these are great! I've never received a present from a man…except Dad and my brother Bill. Many thanks!"

"Well," he said proudly, relieved that she took the gift in the spirit it was given, "I thought you might like some jewelry that was tacky terrific. I figured these huge plastic ear-bobs might be just the thing to complete your stunning outfit!"

"Wow! I should wear them to class on Tuesday," she said holding one up to her ear. "Wouldn't my students be impressed? They might even begin to think that stuffy Dr. Taylor has a sense of humor, after all. Just so they don't think I'll become soft on my grading. Thanks so much, Paul, that was very sweet. These will certainly ensure that I'll always remember tonight…regardless of the game's outcome."

The two finally passed through the metal detectors and ticket takers, then met inside the arena.

"I'm so nervous about the game, I can't believe it," Jordan admitted. "This weekend has been such a great experience for me. I've become, again, the rabid fan of my youth! And now we have to face DUKE! Those Blue Devils are always a talented, well-coached bunch. Of course, how can the Boilers lose now? I'm wearing my lucky earrings!"

"Well," Paul smiled, enjoying the vision of a happy, excited Jordan, "I guess they wouldn't dare lose with you as their new #1 fan."

"Thanks, again, for these lovely, under-stated baubles, Paul," Jordan smiled, swinging her left earring coquettishly with her finger, "and for a wonderful weekend. I'll see you back in Okemos. Sometime, I'd like to talk with you more about your kids' basketball program. Maybe I can help you, in some way."

"You are most welcome, Jordan," Paul responded, "but it is I who must thank you for not making me spend the entire weekend alone! I had a great time, too. And yes, let's do hook up sometime to chat about kids' hoops. I sure hope those lucky earrings do the trick tonight! Go Boilers!"

With that, the two separated to watch what turned out to be another agonizingly close game. By the end, Jordan had completely lost her voice from cheering and screaming with the Purdue crowd. But the earrings worked! Purdue and the Big Ten emerged victorious. Jordan clapped, cheered, hugged those around her and even shed a tear as the coaches and players cut down the net. What an amazing experience. Jordan really didn't think she'd need the earrings to remember this weekend. On the contrary, she was quite sure – this was a weekend she would never forget!

In fact, the week-end in Detroit just might mark a new beginning for the now "friends," who had started off so awkwardly in the fall. Perhaps March Madness would prove to be the start of a genuine, lasting friendship. Neither dared think beyond that possibility. But, just maybe, there was One who might have another plan for the two of them. Only time would tell. Would they ever – could they ever – agree to give love a chance, after all?

CHAPTER TWENTY-ONE

Paul had a late afternoon meeting with Peg to discuss the status of the basketball league while the twins were in their Tai Chi class. This time they opted to meet in the school's small conference room.

"How was the Final Four, Paul?" asked Mrs. Mahoney as they walked toward the conference room.

"It was a memorable week-end, Peg, even though my friend's team lost," said Paul. Entering the conference room, he pulled out a chair for Peg and settled into a seat across the table. "The Governors' event was a lot of fun, and the basketball was terrific even for an addict like me. But the best part…and you'll never believe it…was the friendship that started to develop between Jordan and me. I can hardly believe it, myself!"

"Jordan? That certainly is a surprise!" Peg said, trying to keep her mouth from dropping open. "I guess Ian did mention that she was going to Detroit for the tournament, but how in the world did the two of you hook up?"

"We met accidentally at the Friday night function and ended up sharing a table. Then when we discovered we were staying about a block away from each other, I asked to walk her home. Actually, it turned out to be a power-walk that winded us both," he said laughingly. "Then, on Sunday, since both of our roommates were tied up with the tourney, we decided to take the special, five-hour, city tour. We ended the afternoon with some awesome pizza in Greek Town."

"I'm glad the two of you are becoming friends," Peg said, sincerely. She thought to herself how sometimes just plain guy-gal friendships were just as important as soulmate-relationships. "Now then," continued his willing volunteer, "let's talk about your basketball league. What more needs to be done?"

Paul went on to report that he was surprised how well things had been coming together. The good news was that there were eight schools committed to the program. Actually, it was seven schools and a team composed of several home-schoolers forming the eighth. The first team to sign up was, of course, the Ojibwa Montessori team – followed by the other private Montessori School in the area. Two Montessori programs from Lansing made it four. Three parochial schools plus the home-schooler team completed the list.

"How in the world did you pull off getting the home-schoolers on board, since even identifying them was next to impossible? Somebody must have given you a magic wand," laughed Peg, shaking her head in disbelief.

Paul laughed with her, "Actually, you're right…it was a Fairy Godmother who came to my rescue…in the person of Tammy Sue Randolph. She was determined to get the information I needed. But more than that, she persisted until she figured out how the whole home-school network functions. She came up with information about the key organizers in Ingham County and invited them for coffee. I guess her sticky buns sold them on my idea. It was really very nice of her."

"That's quite a contribution!" Peg paused as a sly smile crossed her lips. "Okay, forgive me, but I can't help asking… is there something brewing between the two of you? I know you've been hoping to find someone to spend time with on a…shall we say…regular basis."

Paul had to smile at Peg's intuition about his intentions. He chuckled, then tried to explain what had been going on between them. When he first met Tammy Sue, they seemed to have a lot in common, and they enjoyed going to some pre-Christmas events together. In fact, they had seen quite a bit of each other in December, and then she went with him to school's basketball outing in January.

"Yes," Peg said, "we enjoyed meeting her after the game, although we really didn't get much of a chance to talk."

"I'm very fond of Tammy," Paul continued, "and for a while I thought that perhaps the relationship would develop into something deeper. But it really never happened. I wasn't sure how she felt about me, either. But, fortunately, it all worked out for the best."

"Okay, Paul…you can't just leave me just hanging. What happened?" she persisted.

Paul laughed, again, warmed that his friend Peg cared so much. He then described for her what had gone on. It turned out that once again, it was the Singles Can group that helped them both avoid an awkward "relationship disaster." It turned out that there were two good-looking men who joined the church group early in the year. Both immediately showed an interest in Tammy Sue, and she in them. One, ironically, had worked with her at Coke in Atlanta. The other had moved to Michigan to take a position at the local newspaper. His uncle was in management at Gannett.

"Tammy Sue thought there might be an opportunity there for her sister's new business," Paul explained. "Both were good guys, and, as it turned out, each of them had more in common with her and her family than I did. I'm just an ordinary guy who enjoys working with little kids and loves basketball. Tammy and I have settled into a comfortable 'friend' relationship. We even went for coffee last week, and she literally glowed as told me all about her old friend from Atlanta, whom she's been seeing quite regularly."

"Wow," Peg nodded, "you and Tammy Sue certainly managed to dodge an uncomfortable bullet, then, I'd say. I'm glad you're still friends and that she is continuing to help with the basketball league. So, what's next for me to do? Will the teams have special names?"

"Of course, you'd ask that question, Peg," Paul smiled. "I was just thinking about that last night, and I came up with an idea I wanted to run by you. What do you think about naming the teams after jungle cats. We could call them unusual names like: lynx, bobcats, panthers, cheetahs, leopards, puma, jaguars and ocelots? We could add an educational component to our program by having the kids do some research on those animals, as well."

"What a great idea, Paul," she agreed, "and the kids will love it!" Peg said she would check with the school secretary about where she usually ordered t-shirts for the school's annual 5-K Run and offered to do the ordering, once she had numbers, colors and sizes. She asked if there were any other tasks she could tackle at the moment.

Paul said he would keep her offer in mind as things progressed. Then they both got up and headed out of the conference room. Peg picked the kids up from Tai Chi and headed home. She listened and asked questions as they eagerly told her about their lesson and what had happened at school that day. It warmed her heart to have these conversations with these two little ones each day. Once again, she paused to mentally pinch herself at how different her life was today, compared to last year. She could hardly remember what she'd done with her time, before the children became such a big part of it.

Peg was eager to tell Ian her news about Paul and Jordan. For someone who hadn't considered herself a gossip, she'd certainly picked up some interesting news that afternoon. Maybe, it wasn't gossip if she only shared it with her spouse. After all, they both cared about Paul and Jordan.

Later that night, after the children were settled in their beds and the couple was finally alone, Peg began telling Ian all about Paul's weekend in Detroit. But, as it turned out, she wasn't the only one who had that story. Ian told his wife that he was quite surprised when Jordan came into the lab that day. She had actually told him a similar story. Although she'd been careful not to suggest there was anything between Paul and herself, Ian told Peg he thought he'd noticed a lilt to her voice, as Jordan described their time together.

They chatted about how funny life could be. After all, who would have predicted their journey over the past year. They remembered last fall, when they had asked Jordan and Paul to dinner, thinking it would be nice for two young people, both new to the area, to meet one another. Then the evening had turned awkward, when Jordan left abruptly. Things had been going so well, they remembered, until Paul mentioned the Singles Can group at church and suggested they go together. Was it the "church" or Paul's suggestion of a "date?" They were still confused about what had scared Jordan away.

"Well," Ian said, "basketball was the topic that seemed to connect the two of them at the dinner…at least until Jordan's abrupt departure. So, it makes sense that basketball would be the common thread that could connect the two of them, again."

Peg and Ian agreed that a shared love of basketball seemed to have eased their first awkward encounter and enabled them to form a tentative truce. This time, they even seemed to have enjoyed each other's company. Ian told Peg that he had secretly hoped that someone like Paul would find a way to break down Jordan's hostility toward eligible men. After all, he cared about his former student and knew that the trauma of her college years had somehow been blocking her ability to trust others – or maybe trust herself. Peg suggested that perhaps the Detroit weekend had created a small crack in the wall Jordan had built around her feelings. The good news was that Jordan wanted to become involved with the youth basketball program Paul was creating. That opened many possibilities.

"Two people, working together toward a common goal of helping others…well, that's powerful medicine," Ian mused, aloud. "Just look what happened to us when we agreed to co-lead the Chapel's youth group." They looked at each other and smiled. Yes, that was powerful medicine, indeed.

CHAPTER TWENTY-TWO

Jordan was eager to get back to East Lansing after her fabulous time in Detroit. She had a wonderful chat with Martha when she went over to thank her for loaning her the jewelry and purse. Jordan gave her friend a detailed account of the short holiday.

"You were so right about going," Jordan said appreciatively. "In fact, you were right about everything. My outfit for the gala was perfect and made me feel so special. It reminded me of when I was a girl and my dad used to call me, 'Princess.' And getting to know Paul as a friend, rather than a suitor, was an unexpected bonus. Thank you for everything, Martha."

Martha listened carefully and nodded. Then she offered, "I'm glad you went, Jordan, and I'm delighted that you had a chance to get to know Paul as a friend. Friendship with someone of the opposite gender can often be meaningful... and sometimes far less stressful than a romantic relationship." How wise she was!

Things on campus had begun to move quickly. Members of the team that had been in Mozambique were excited about how much had been accomplished. They were confident that identifying key farmers and helping them become mentors for their neighbors was certain to result in a higher level of production for all involved. Dana and the U. S. Attaché had also been successful in obtaining governmental commitment to support one – or possibly two, small, biodiesel processing plants which would produce fuel to meet local needs. This year's projected Jatropha yields would provide ample feedstock for those processing plants. After careful inspection, it was also determined that the road infrastructure in the designated area would be adequate for the near future.

Further, the team had engaged in a number of positive discussions with both individual and co-op farmers about the idea of contract farming to ensure a market for their Jatropha crops. Already successful contracting for local cotton and tobacco had provided both a model and an incentive for farmers to pursue contracting for Jatropha crops, as well.

After leaving the team to their work in the lab, Dana asked to meet privately with Ian. He led her to his office, and they sat down to chat.

Dana began, "I really wanted to talk to you about something, Ian." She hesitated, then said slowly, "I have to admit, I was more than a little worried about Chris's behavior on the trip." She hesitated, again, then plunged on. "He seemed distracted, and I don't know--'contemplative'--might be the best word to describe it. His demeanor seemed to change after he spent some time with Pastor John, the person who came to visit the Okemos Chapel. Perhaps, it was nothing, but I thought I should mention it. When I asked him if everything was okay, he looked surprised that I would even ask. But, then, he continued to act strangely."

"Thank you for telling me, Dana," Ian said appreciatively. "I hope it's nothing, but I'll keep my eyes and ears open and see if he displays any concerning behavior, now that he's back here. Again, I appreciate you letting me know that something might be amiss. By the way, you did a fabulous job in Mozambique. I could not be prouder of all you and the others were able to accomplish in such a short time."

Dana beamed at the praise, as she went back to join the team.

After she left, Ian reflected on her concerns about Christian. He had some notion about what might be causing the young man's behavior, but he had decided not to share his hunch.

Things were very busy in the lab that week. Everyone was glad to be back, and the entire team shared renewed energy and optimism for the project. Over the next few days, Ian couldn't help but notice a change in Jordan. She was focused on her work, as always, but at the same time, she seemed almost – light-hearted! He even thought he might have overheard her – humming!

When they met in the lab a few days later, Ian said, "I'm glad you were able to get away over the weekend, Jordan. I think the break was good for you…you certainly deserved it, after all the long hours you'd been putting in lately. I'm glad you had such a good time."

"It was certainly wonderful to see my old roommate, and great to re-connect with Paul, too," she said breezily.

"Well, roommates are special friends, that's for sure," he agreed, "and I'm glad that you and Paul had a chance to spend some time together, too."

"So am I." She sighed, then went on, "In retrospect, the awkwardness with Paul was all my fault, really. Except for my dad, you and my brother, I've never really felt at ease with a man. But over the week-end, I came to understand that Paul Franklin is a nice fellow and very easy to be around. I realized that I could have a 'male friend' without thinking of him as a 'suitor.' In the long run, that may be best…at least for me."

"Well that's great, Jordan," Ian said encouragingly. "Peg and I think the world of Paul. He's considerate, creative, generous; he loves kids, and he has a great sense of humor. Plus…as my wife doesn't hesitate to remind me…he can cook! That sounds like a great 'male friend' for you to have!"

They both laughed at the "good cook" comment and then turned their attention to research matters.

Ian was eager to get Jordan's reaction to what was a tiny – but possibly-important breakthrough in her research. He and David had been in the lab over the week-end, when one of the landscapers conducting field trials on her grass had called. He reported that the trial plots had been planted and were – in his astonished words – "growing like weeds!"

They both had a chuckle over the landscaper's use of words. Then Jordan confessed, "That's great news, Ian. I wasn't expecting an immediate result. I'll remain skeptical, but optimistic and see what happens. I have to admit, I'm a little envious of that landscaper. I still get a kick out of feeling the warm, moist soil on my hands when I'm setting out plants. Looking at test vials or checking results in the lab is exciting, but I don't get the same emotional reaction that digging in the dirt gives me. It's hard to forget how much I enjoyed my first job with the landscape firm back home in Indiana."

"I don't think any of us can forget that 'first job.'" Ian agreed. "There's something about doing a job that's challenging and fulfilling for the very first time…and getting paid to do it."

Changing the subject, Ian said, "Jordan, how well have you gotten to know Dana?"

"Pretty well, I guess," Jordan replied thinking about the numerous conversations she'd had with the young grad student.

Ian continued his thought, "From your perspective, where

do you think she should be heading, professionally? She's certainly bright enough to pursue a doctorate, but I wonder if that's the right choice for her? I worry that sometimes we push some of our students in that direction because they have research ability, instead of focusing on what's the best career choice for a particular student." The professors were both silent thinking about Ian's concern.

"I see what you mean," said his thoughtful colleague. "In Dana's case, I suspect her interest lies in the policy area. She really enjoys talking about the challenges of mediating intellectual disagreements, coming up with compromises and managing multi-faceted projects. She found her work with Washington legislators to be especially fulfilling. I understand she felt the same way negotiating with politicians about issues in Mozambique. I heard her say that politicians all over the world are quite similar…they want what's best for their constituents, but they all have to juggle conflicting needs. And…of course…some are corrupt. I think that she'll make the right decision about a doctorate, all on her own."

"Yes, of course, you're right. She's a young woman who knows her own mind and has pretty clear goals, I suspect," Ian concurred. "I don't think we'll try to persuade her one way or the other."

Nodding, Jordan changed the subject. "Now, sir, it's time to get a look at what's happening in the lab."

They both knew that while they were making significant progress on their research, real success was still a long way off and would be more difficult once David Mason graduated and left the team. Jordan wondered how and when the breakthrough would come. For her, it was not a matter of "if" but "when."

Ian felt the same way. He couldn't help but wonder if the

research going on in Japan would be a key to unlocking this genetic dilemma. Just perhaps, his dad's connection with his Japanese neighbor might turn up a clue – or even Jordan's contact with the new Japanese bio-chemistry professor. If they were able to understand what the Japanese research on Jatropha was uncovering – perhaps they could combine their findings to arrive at a solution more quickly. Wouldn't it be great if scientists from two countries could come together to assist the people of a third. Perhaps, together they could help Mozambican farmers increase both the quantity and quality of oilseeds produced by their sometimes-pesky, fast-growing Jatropha weed! It was his dream that he and his team would be part of making that happen…and to realize that dream, he could use all the help he could get!

CHAPTER TWENTY-THREE

Jordan gave Paul a call and arranged to meet him at Ojibwa to discuss his remaining issues concerning the basketball league and tournament he'd scheduled for early July. When he'd called her earlier, he confirmed that he had eight teams participating and that both boys and girls would be involved. He still had a couple of issues to be resolved, though, and he hoped she would be able to help him figure it all out. She wondered what the issues could be, since he seemed very organized and resourceful. At 5 o'clock, she dashed home from the office, donned a jogging suit and athletic shoes and headed to the school. When she arrived, she saw Paul dressed in similar garb. Perhaps they could shoot a few hoops in the school's gym before their meeting.

"Hey, Paul, do you have any basketballs around here… and do we have time to shoot a few before we get to work?" she suggested.

Paul looked surprised, but a smile quickly filled his face. "Fine with me, lady. You're on!"

He led her to the equipment room and grabbed a couple of balls. After dribbling around and shooting a few warmup shots, Jordan challenged Paul to a game of "one-on-one."

Paul gleefully accepted the challenge, "You really want to challenge me? Well, okay, I wouldn't mind kicking your rear in my own gym."

Jordan grabbed the basketball, dribbled up the court and threw in a layup, before Paul could even react. Evenly matched? You'd better believe it! After fifteen minutes of racing back and forth on the half-court, there was a disagreement about the score. Each thought he/she was up by two. Finally, two exhausted ex-basketball champs called the afternoon's match a tie. They both grabbed their water bottles and collapsed on the floor. Chests heaving, they looked at one another fiercely…then began laughing.

"Hey," Jordan said, "you're not half bad. But…just 'who kicked who's rear?' is what I want to know?"

"Okay, okay," Paul said, raising his hands in defeat, "I demand a rematch. You tricked me with that early layup… and who could believe a little girl like you could launch the three-ball like that?"

"Little girl, huh? Want a rematch right now?" she asked, defiantly.

"Well, I would…." Paul stammered, "but we have work to do! Let's replay this game later."

"Deal," Jordan agreed triumphantly.

Standing, he pulled Jordan to her feet, and the two headed toward the conference room.

"So," asked Jordan after collapsing in a comfortable chair, "what're the big problems we have to solve?"

Paul sat down across from her and began, "As I mentioned on the phone, both boys and girls are going to be playing in the league and tourney. It's wonderful that the little girls want to play, but it's something I hadn't anticipated at their age. I'm all for Title IX, but we don't have enough kids to field separate teams…at least not this first year."

"That is a problem, Paul," she responded. "Now, tell me again, how many kids will be on each team?"

"Well, I thought it would work, if we had ten or twelve

per team. Do you think that'll be enough? Hey, by the way, do you happen to have a nick-name?"

"When we were kids my brother, Bill, called me 'Jordie' as a way to get even when I called him 'Willie Wonka.' Actually, Jordie is fine with me. In fact, I kind of like it." She warmed at the idea of a nickname, then went on. "So, are the numbers of boys and girls about even on each team? I mean, can you recruit as many girls as boys?"

"I think so, looking at the names of those who have registered already...although I'm not certain, and kids are still signing up," he explained.

"I have a couple more questions, Mr. Ex-Hawk," Jordan went on. "Didn't you say these kids would range from five to eight or nine years old? That's quite a difference in size, large-motor development and ability, I'd think. And if you throw in gender differences, you're talking quite a range. Were you considering mixed teams? I know they do that with some sports...like softball and soccer...but basketball?"

"That's my biggest concern!" Paul admitted. "That's what I was hoping you could help me with."

Paul went on to explain that there were some significant size and ability differences among the kids, even at the same age. The Mahoney twins were a prime example of that. Mike was certainly a lot taller and stronger than petite little Mia, but she seemed more feisty and perhaps more coordinated and competitive than her brother. "We can't ignore safety and liability issues," the program's administrator stated.

"I really don't think you should have mixed boy/girl teams. It's a little too risky. Some of the little girls could literally be run over by the bigger boys. It's already complicated by the wide age discrepancy. I have an idea, though, if you're open to changing a few rules," Jordan offered.

At his nod, she went on to explain her idea, which she

thought of when he mentioned Michael Mahoney. During the women's game at Breslin, Mike had observed that the women played four quarters instead of two halves like the men. What if, in this league, they played four, shortened quarters, like in the women's games? That way they could alternate quarters – girls could play in quarters one and three, the boys in two and four. Paul was silent for a moment, working it out in his mind. She also thought the coaches would have to be sure to field players of similar skills levels at the same time – keeping the big kids from dominating the game. Perhaps that could be done by having frequent time-outs to change lineups – similar to line changes in hockey.

"What a great idea, Jordie!" Paul said enthusiastically. "That also solves another issue. There's really no reason that both genders have to have exactly the same number of participants, as long as all who sign up get about the same amount of playing time. So, since we'll be rotating kids in and out, we can actually have more kids on each team. There's no reason to limit signups. I was a little worried about what would happen if we had too many kids for one team, but not enough for two. This plan gives us lots of flexibility. Yes, I think it could work."

Paul realized that this solution also posed the need for him to rethink the rules of the game. He certainly valued Jordan's perspective, so he suggested that he would draft a new set of rules and asked Jordan if she'd look them over and provide feedback. She nodded her agreement, flattered that he sought her opinion so openly.

"Well, now that that's solved, are you ready for another round of b-ball, Jordie…or shall we continue our problem-solving effort?" her host wanted to know.

Jordan took a deep breath, "The heart is willing but not the arms and legs. What's next on the agenda, Franklin?"

Paul was half-kidding about another game, anyway. He really wanted to get these issues resolved today.

Paul admitted to Jordan that he really had no experience when it came to either recruiting or training referees. He'd often found plenty to criticize about their calls and even joked about taking salary deductions when wrong calls were made – but how to organize a bunch of volunteer refs? That was beyond his skill-set. He wondered if Jordan had any suggestions on how to tackle the issue of game officials.

Once again, Jordan came to his rescue. She responded with a big smile and said in jest, "Funny you should ask… part of the answer is sitting across the table from you. Guess what? I'm a certified referee for high school girls' basketball in Texas, and I'm in the process of getting certified in Michigan. So, voila! I could be your ref trainer. When it comes to recruiting, though…no way! I really don't have that kind of network here, so I can't help you with that."

"Hot diggity dog!" Paul gushed. "You sure are a God-send, Jordie! When in the world did you have time to do all that? You're certainly full of surprises, my friend."

The lady referee took her time to explain. She told him that when she was in high school, she had earned National Honor Society points by reffing in the intramural and summer youth basketball programs. Then, while at A & M, she'd noticed a poster in the union seeking referees for women's games. She'd seized that opportunity as a way to increase her income and provide a break from her rigorous studies. However, what actually happened had a much bigger payoff. She easily passed the written certification exam but had failed the skill test. Jordan admitted to Paul that she had gained a lot of weight, was totally out-of-shape and could not meet the physical requirements for certification.

"And, so," she said defiantly, "I got busy at the gym. I lost weight, built up my stamina and regained my playing-form. When I retook the skill test, I passed it with ease, and thus started my career as a striped shirt. I worked in a series of summer basketball camps for girls. Later, I actually officiated a number of high school games...much to my brother's surprise and concern. He was afraid I might show up someday to officiate one of his boys' games."

It totally surprised her that she had confessed this personal story to this particular man. She thought that Ian had probably wondered about her weight loss, but, of course, had never asked about it. It was quite unusual for her to reveal parts of her past to others. And it was a totally new experience for her to place this kind of trust in someone she didn't know all that well and certainly hadn't considered to be a friend – until very recently.

"Wow, Jordie," Paul said, looking at her with admiration, "you are one, amazing woman...chock full of surprises. So, how do we go about recruiting refs? I'm not sure where we should even begin looking." He paused, then snapped his fingers. "I know, maybe the Mahoneys, Allens and Lanes could help us recruit."

"Good idea, Paul. They've been in the community longer than either of us," she noted. "Of course, parents are always willing to volunteer. But I suspect they'd make better timers and score-keepers...thus avoiding any temptation to favor their children or their children's teams."

"I think we'll need two refs for each game. I'd like to pair a male and female, if possible," Paul said.

The more they brain-stormed, the more ideas for ref recruiting occurred to them. Paul said that members of the Singles Can group were always looking for ways to get involved in the community. They might enjoy learning a new set of skills and getting a workout without going to a health club. He also thought of former basketball players in the area who might enjoy working with kids. Jordan suggested high-schoolers, perhaps looking for Honor Society points like she did or other volunteer opportunities to enhance their college applications. Paul agreed and thought Libby Lane might know some kids who would be interested. Staff members at the participating schools was another resource. This was going to be a 5-9-year-old league, after all...not the NBA, so the time commitment wouldn't be that great. The best thing to do, they agreed, was to keep the training and scheduling simple.

Moving to the last issue on his list, Paul said, "I was also thinking, it might also be a good idea to have some kind of medical personnel on hand for the tournament. I can just see a little one turning an ankle or breaking an arm. It could certainly happen with so many kids playing. Perhaps one of Peg's friends, Jodie or Ben Allen, would be willing to serve as an on-site medical person...or perhaps Jodie can get other nurses to help. I'll bet Dr. Wang, the Tai Chi instructor here at Ojibwa, would also take a turn. If we had several volunteers, no one would have to be there all day."

"I hadn't thought of that, Paul, but you're right," Jordie agreed. "It's not so much the liability...it's the peace of mind knowing someone's there who can handle a medical emergency."

Gathering his papers, Paul stood up. "Hey, Jordie, thanks so much for all your ideas, today...you've really helped me out," Paul said gratefully. "As a thank-you, how about joining me for some homemade minestrone soup, I've had simmering in the slow cooker all day? It's so late now, I hate to make you go home and begin making dinner for yourself. I can throw together an antipasto salad, too."

"Sounds like good eating to me," Jordan said, suddenly

ravenously hungry. "As you've probably guessed, culinary art is not really my thing." Then she added quickly, "Of course, I can pull together a simple healthy meal, when necessary. After all, anyone can read a recipe! Shall I pick up something for dessert?"

"Thanks, but there's no need," Paul said. "I always have a supply of spumoni ice cream in the freezer. See you in… say…half an hour? Here's my address. Again, Jordan, thanks so much for your help this afternoon. I have to admit, I really struck gold when you offered to help!"

Jordan smiled, "Okay, Paul, see you soon!" Jordan headed for her car, wondering if she had time for a quick shower.

On the drive home, Dr. Taylor assured herself that this was not going to be a "date." It was just a causal meal after a productive late-afternoon meeting. Today it had just been two friends – working on a project of mutual interest. She was looking forward to dinner, though, she had to admit.

Paul's Italian dishes were delicious, and the conversation went well beyond kid's basketball leagues. They found themselves chatting easily and naturally about each other's pasts and current interests. Jordan told Paul about her love of gardening and how she thought she'd hate being cooped up in an apartment or condo. Paul told Jordan about his dream of building his own house on a spacious lot with enough space for privacy and a big yard for kids someday. Since both Jordan and Paul were the younger kids in their families, they shared several hilarious stories about baiting their older siblings. Paul said he'd teased his sister with mice that he'd caught, and Jordan admitted listening in on her brother's phone calls with a bevy of girls who liked having a basketball player for a boyfriend.

Neither noticed how quickly the time passed. Suddenly, Jordan noticed her watch – it was close to 10 o'clock! Jordan helped clean up the kitchen, then turned to leave.

"Thanks so much for dinner, Paul, it was great!" Jordan said sincerely.

She walked toward the door, then turned back and surprising herself, she added, "If you have the rule proposal ready by the end of the week, why don't you email it to me? Then, perhaps you can come over this weekend to go over it. We can have something…say…Mexican for lunch. How does that sound?"

"You're on," he responded enthusiastically. "I'll get busy on the rules tomorrow and shoot them to you, as soon as I'm done…and I love Mexican, by the way…actually I like all food!"

They smiled as they parted…no awkwardness between them, just an easy familiarity. Little did the Italian chef know that his hostess had already mentally cased the Mexican "joints" in town and planned to order take-out. As the day drew to a close, both friends were pleased with their productive and enjoyable time together – and both found themselves looking forward to the weekend.

CHAPTER TWENTY-FOUR

Spring was in the air, and Mia and Mike were eager to again participate in Small Animal's Day on campus. How they loved touring the barns and seeing the wooly baby lambs! Peg and Ian remembered how much they had enjoyed the day last year – and the dozens of questions the kids had asked. Peg also remembered that it was this event last year that had prompted her to invite the Mahoneys to the farm to meet her parents. She smiled as she recalled how excited the twins were to see the two new colts. When her parents invited the kids to actually name the colts, they were over-the-moon. What priceless memories for all of them!

Driving around the university farms on a bright spring day and seeing all the baby animals was fun for all four of them, but the kids couldn't stop talking about "Mommy's farm." They knew they'd be going there the following weekend, and they couldn't wait. Although they'd seen G-ma and Papa G a couple of times since Christmas, this would be their first visit to the farm since the holidays.

"Do you think there'll be any new colts for us to name this year, Mikey?" asked his horse-loving sister.

"Don't be silly, Mia. Of course, there will!" he responded adamantly. "Spring is when babies are born on the farm... you know that! And I'm sure it'll be our job to name them."

"Well, we sure did a good job last year," Mia said, proudly.

"Lady Long Legs and Tornado were perfect names. I wonder how big they are now? Naming a colt's a whole lot easier than naming a baby, I bet."

The family arrived at the farm late Saturday morning. The kids jumped out of the car and ran into their grandparents' arms. After hugs, all around, they all went into the house for a country meal. Although it was just an ordinary Saturday, G-ma had fixed fried chicken with all of the trimmings for her daughter's family. The kids (and their parents) sopped up the last of the gravy, just as Papa G produced a big tub of home-made ice cream for dessert. Although they protested that they were way too full, they all managed to down bowls of the frosty confection, anyway.

After the noon meal, the kids hurried into the farmyard to play with the dog – throwing balls and sticks that were eagerly retrieved by the wagging canine. Once the grownups had finished cleaning up the kitchen, they emerged from the backdoor, and Papa G announced it was time to check to see if there was a new colt. The fact that one had arrived earlier in the week had been kept secret from the children.

The kids raced ahead to the paddock and climbed onto the wooden slats of the fence. Sure enough, there was one, spindly-legged colt standing next to its mother.

"Oh, he's beautiful!" gasped Mia reverently. "Is it a boy or a girl, Papa?"

"It's a male, Honey," responded her grandfather, "and he was just born on Tuesday, so he's really new."

"Wow," whispered Mike, under his breath. "He watched as the little foal sidled up to his mother, looking for milk."

"Do you think you two might be able to come up with a name for this little fellow?" asked their granddad.

"Oh, Papa G," said Michael excitedly, "you know we can!"

"This is going to be hard!" said Mia turning to her brother

with a perplexed frown on her face. "This foal has no special markings or his body, Mikey."

"That's true," he agreed.

Just then, the colt turned to look at the little cluster of people by the fence. They all got a clear view of his face.

"Look, Mia!" exclaimed Mike, "Do you see that white zig-zag on his forehead? It kind of looks like a flash of lightening or a streak of fire."

The kids tossed around several ideas based on the zig-zag marking. Then Mia called everyone to attention.

"I have an idea," she suggested, "let's have a tribal council. Then, everybody gets a vote."

The kids announced their name choices. It was a tough decision. On the first ballot – there were two votes for Lightning, two for Blaze, and two for Flash. The group debated the names, each giving reasons for his or her favorite. Then, they took a second vote. This time the vote was three for Lightning, three for Blaze, and zero for Flash. Since the group was still divided, G-ma suggested that Mike and Mia make the final decision.

They whispered for a moment, then Michael announced, "His name is Lightning."

Everyone cheered. Then they went over to another paddock, and Papa G put a harness on Lady Long Legs. Each twin took a turn leading the yearling around the lot with Papa and Dad close by. The adventuresome Mia begged to sit on "her" special horse for a minute – just to see what it felt like. She knew that Lady loved her so much, she wouldn't mind if her special friend got to sit on her back for a little bit. Grandddad didn't think it was such a good idea, but the little miss continued to plead and even shed a few tears. So, finally, the men relented and lifted her carefully onto the horse's back. NOT A GOOD DECISION!

In that single moment, the horse was spooked by a garter snake that nobody had seen in the grass. In spite of the precautions taken, the little rider fell hard onto the ground, hit her head and landed awkwardly. She was still for a moment, her leg in a clearly painful position. Then she started moaning pitifully. Soon, both she and her twin were in tears. The adults rushed to her side. G-ma grabbed a nearby piece of fencing and ripped off her scarf. They quickly immobilized her leg, then her father gently lifted her, and they moved swiftly to the car.

Pete, Peg and Ian took Mia to the hospital, while Michael stayed at the farm with his grandmother. In the emergency room, the doctor quickly confirmed a broken leg, several cracked ribs and the possibility of a concussion. After ordering an MRI to confirm there was no cranial damage and setting Mia's lower leg in a bright blue cast, the doctor assured the distraught parents that Mia would be just fine.

Talk about shock, guilt and embarrassment!

Back at the farm, Michael was frantic about the well-being of his twin. He worried that she was hurt badly and may not be able to run and play – her leg looked so scary! There were so many things for a five-year-old to understand – so many questions to be answered. G-ma tried to patiently reassure the little boy and distract him while the others headed to the hospital. G-ma and Mike were both relieved when Ian called to let them know the doctor had seen Mia and put a cast on her leg. He said he would call later with further updates, but not to worry.

The attending physician told the waiting parents and grandfather that although the little girl would be fine, it would take time for the leg to heal. Fortunately, it had been a clean break and at her age, it would heal quickly. Her ribs would continue to be sore for a week or two, but they should heal quickly, as well. He wanted to keep Mia at the hospital over the weekend for observation.

"I didn't see any damage on her cranial scan," the doctor reported, "but I'd like to monitor her for a possible concussion and keep her very quiet so the healing process can begin. You parents are welcome to spend the night in her room, if you'd like. Her brother and grandparents can visit tomorrow."

What an unexpected turn of events. The next day, Mikey walked slowly into the hospital to see his twin. It was scary, especially when he saw her in her hospital bed. But once he noticed that Mia was bright, cheerful and eager to tell her brother all about her hospital adventure, Michael finally relaxed. He even signed her cast and drew a big smiley face on it. He was fascinated by all of the apparatus they had in her room to make sure she was doing okay. He left her reluctantly with his grandparents but promised he'd see her at the farm the following day.

Being treated like an only child was a new experience for Mike. Papa G took him out to the paddock to see the horses. He explained that animals – even tame ones, are unpredictable. That's why it's so important to always be careful around them. He reassured the little boy that Lady did not mean to throw Mia. It was the snake that had spooked her. Michael felt better after seeing the horses calmly munching grass in the field. He decided he would be sure to let Mia know that Lady Long Legs was still his sister's special friend.

After returning to the farm to collect their luggage, Mia asked if she could go see Lady Long Legs. Of course, she was unable to walk on the uneven ground, but Papa G solved the problem by letting her ride beside him on his Gator. Arriving at the field, Mia quickly spotted Lady Long Legs munching away at the far end of the field. To her surprise, Lady wandered over to the fence, when Papa G called her. Then he gave her a cube of sugar.

"She doesn't look scared, now, Papa," Mia said calmly. "I felt so sorry for her, when she jumped. I know she must have been really frightened."

"Well, we all learned a good lesson this weekend," he said. "No more sitting on horses without helmets, for one thing. And no more riding horses that haven't been trained. Don't worry, though, my little horse-lover, you'll have plenty of time to ride again. But next time, we'll all be a little more careful."

That afternoon, the family made the return trip to Okemos. At Dr. Allen's suggestion, they went directly to a new Rehab Center that had a special wing for children. Ben and Jodie met them there and provided a reassuring diagnosis after examining the little patient.

"Mia's bones will heal quickly, but we need to begin therapy tomorrow morning. That's why I recommend that she stay here for the balance of the week," Dr. Ben explained. "While she did black out for a short time, there was no actual concussion according to the tests they ran at the hospital. Starting tomorrow, she will have therapy for short intervals several times a day for the rest of the week. Being here will lessen the need to move her. Because of the injury to her ribs, she's unable to use crutches right now and moving her in and out of a car with her leg cast would be quite painful. While she's not in danger, it would be best for her to remain here, until those ribs have a chance to begin healing."

Jodie took over from her husband, "I've called the Lanes, Ida and also Paul and Jordan. We all want to help. You may both want to spend afternoons and early evenings with Mia here at the Rehab Center. As Ben said, her therapy will take place throughout the day, so you'll be able to watch when you're here. Ben will check on her progress daily, of course."

Ben added, "I know the Rehab Center is new for Mia, so if one of you would like to stay with her tonight…or any night…you're welcome."

It was decided that Peg would sleep in the recliner that night, keeping her little girl company.

Daddy took their tired son home and spent time talking with him about all that had happened that weekend. Michael was still a little scared but talking with Daddy made everything seem – almost normal. Prayers were very special that Monday night. Mike and Dad were at peace knowing that God and Dr. Ben were in charge of little Mia.

After Michael was asleep, Ian lugged suitcases upstairs and began unpacking. Just then, his phone buzzed.

"Hello there, Ian…so sorry to hear about Mia's accident." The voice on the other end of the line was that of Paul Franklin. "Jodie called and told me about what happened. I'm so sorry! I just wanted to report that I have a sub for Peg tomorrow morning. Also, I'm going to be Michael's buddy after school tomorrow and will feed him and keep him here 'til you can pick him up on your way home. Jordan has made up a schedule for Mikey for the rest of week, until our little horsewoman is home. Also, Jodie contacted Ida and Pastor Becky, who have insisted on providing meals for the rest of the week. They will be in your refrigerator, when you and Peg get home each day."

"Whoa! Thanks so much, Paul! Having friends like you and the others is truly a gift from God," Ian said, feeling a lump form in his throat. "We really do want to spend as much time as we can with Mia. Mikey will want to visit, too, of course. We plan to take turns staying with her during and after dinner until she falls asleep each night, then stopping by each morning before work. Knowing that Michael has special attention, too, will help us all."

So that's how the week unfolded. Peg would head over to the Center after school, then Ian and Mikey would come for a while after Ian got out of work. Peg or Ian would take Mike home, while the other parent stayed until Mia fell asleep. They took turns staying and stopping by in the morning. It was a crazy schedule, and meals for the couple often happened after Mikey's bedtime, but it worked for them.

Meanwhile, on Tuesday, Paul taught young Michael how to play a kid's version of "Horse." Together, they cooked spaghetti and meatballs, and the man gave the boy a first lesson in playing a tune on his keyboard, before Ian picked him up for a visit to the Rehab Center.

Wednesday night was Jordan's turn. She took him swimming at the YMCA, stopped for Tacos and joined Martha for games of Chinese Checkers – a new game for him. Martha delighted at having the youngster visit her home and for Ian to stop by, to pick up his son.

Thursday night Jordie and Paul took Mike to look at the lot Paul was considering buying. It was where he was thinking of building his dream house. Then, it was back to Ottawa Drive for the mac and cheese dinner Ida had prepared for the threesome. After dinner, they went with Mikey to visit Mia, who was looking forward to getting home the next day.

Friday afternoon, Ian, Peg and Mike piled into the car and headed to the Rehab Center to bring Mia home, at last. After signing all the release papers, and pushing her wheelchair to the curb, Ian carefully lifted Mia into the spacious backseat of the car and buckled her in. She chattered on as they made their way home, Mikey alternately asking endless questions and telling his sister all about his week.

After dinner, Jodie, Ben and BJ arrived to pick Mike up. He had been invited for an overnight at the Allens. Being with BJ, Auntie Jo and Uncle Ben was always a treat for the older boy, who adored his young friend and loved playing with his many toys. They also had time to make some special finger paintings to welcome Mia home. After stories, the two boys settled down in BJ's room and fell immediately asleep.

At home, Mia was exhausted, as well. After a fun sponge bath and tooth brushing, she was helped into her very own bed for a story and prayers. She snuggled down under her covers and closed her eyes. Her father sat in a chair beside the bed, watching his little girl relax and drift off to sleep. After kissing her head softly, Ian headed downstairs.

At long last, Peggy and Ian collapsed on the couch and finally had a moment to spend some much-need time, alone. They realized it was something they had missed doing in recent months. While Mia slept, they began talking about the events of the week. Soon, however, their conversation moved to thoughts and concerns about their marriage, their family and the future. Because of the scare with Mia, they had become acutely aware of the fragility of life. They began to wonder, if, perhaps, they had been taking things for granted – especially when it came to their own relationship.

Peg and Ian had to admit they were both surprised and dismayed that they hadn't set aside time for even a few date nights, since their honeymoon, almost a year before. How could that have happened? They remembered how they'd vowed to make time for each other, but the demands of work, family and life in general, had gotten in the way. Somehow, that precious "shared time" they'd promised each other had just not happened. That realization hit them both – very hard.

"I've missed those special intimate conversations we often had after our youth meetings," Ian mused softly.

"As have I," his wife concurred. "Remember those unexpected moments we used to share…like when we tore down Africa after the school's International Night? Even in my grubbies, you took me to lunch at the Purple Carrot, and we went shopping at the Farmers' Market. I remember every single minute of that Saturday afternoon, Dear. I think I knew, even then, that I would love you…regardless of what happened with our relationship. And I'll never forget that romantic dinner at the English Inn…I thought I was the luckiest girl in the world to be with you."

"It was magical for me, too," Ian said, nestling his wife in his arms. "Whatever happened? It's not that we don't talk and share ideas. We do that every night, but it's often about trivial things – not about us! I hate to say it, but I'm afraid like too many couples we got caught up in work, the children's needs, friends and community obligations. We haven't made it a priority to spend time with each other. I plead guilty! It's my fault. I should have been more aware. Can you ever forgive me, my Dear One?"

Peg turned to look at her husband, her eyes glistening, "Oh, Dear, Dear Ian, it's no one's fault! Life happens! I guess that's what it means to be a family! We can't blame or punish ourselves…or each other…for caring about work, our children, friends or the community. That's what makes us who we are…what brought us together."

"Yes, you're right, of course," Ian agreed, "but we never really did much dating, and our engagement period was so short. As good as we are about planning and managing all other aspects of our lives…I guess we should have taken the time to do that with our relationship, too. Well, it's not too late."

He sat up, put his hands on his wife's shoulders, and gazed deeply into her eyes. "Mrs. Mahoney, I hear-by pledge to you…that I will do my part to nurture our love and see it blossom as we grow older together!" And with that, Ian pulled her to him and kissed her deeply.

After a breathless moment, Peg took Ian's face in her hands and pledged, "And I, my Dearest Husband, promise to do the same. Let's vow to go somewhere and do something together, at least two times per month…every month. Whether it's a show or out-to-dinner or simply walking through the campus gardens to smell the roses. From now on…let's make it our number-one priority."

"Agreed," her husband concurred.

It was too bad that it took a potential tragedy to make them stop and consider how precious and fragile life really was. Could it have been, in fact, the Heavenly Father, who'd provided them with a much-needed wake-up call? The Lord sometimes works in mysterious ways to help his children see the light. Tears of thanksgiving fell on both of their cheeks as they murmured a grateful prayer that their little girl was, thankfully, okay, and that they had been given a priceless opportunity to make things right with…and for…each other.

The couple rose and sealed their covenant by holding hands and retiring to the warmth of their bed, together.

CHAPTER TWENTY-FIVE

The Montessori school year was winding down. Everyone was getting excited about the annual International Festival. This year, Miss Peggy's room was being transformed into Asia, Mr. Paul's would become Europe; and the twins couldn't stop talking about Australia. They were delighted to have helped Mrs. H. bake four loaves of Kiwi nut bread as their contribution to the international feast. Peg and Ian recalled with fondness how the previous year they had worked to make an African display which turned out to be a unique experience for visitors of all ages. This year, Christian had been invited to be part of the African exhibit, again; and he was delighted to do it. Once again, the International Festival was a great success. After helping their mother return her room to normalcy, the Mahoney children headed home with their parents – lugging artwork and crafts they had made, trinkets and maps…and, of course, their "passports," which had been stamped at every "continent" room they visited.

Calendars were filling up fast for adults, too, as the end of the school year approached. So, when Ian and Peg proposed a "thank you" dinner at the English Inn for their friends who had done so much to support the family after Mia's fall, they were delighted that both couples were able to attend. Jodie and Ben had spent a lot of time with them and Mia at the Rehab Center, making sure her medical protocol was followed to the letter. Jordan and Paul and the Allens had also gone out of their way to organize meal donations and plan special activities for Michael, while Peg and Ian were with Mia at Center. Without their help, it would have been a very difficult time for the little boy, who had been so concerned about his twin.

As they arrived that Saturday evening, each of the three couples strolled up the winding sidewalk to the ornate doorway of the Inn. They were greeted graciously by the hostess and led to a beautifully appointed, round table by a window overlooking the grounds of the estate. The friends settled into their seats and grabbed their crisp linen napkins, as a solicitous waiter poured water for everyone.

"What a lovely place for dinner on a beautiful spring evening," remarked Jordan. "I can't believe this actual 'English country house' is tucked away on the river…so close to the city. I'm anxious to learn about its history and see the lush gardens up close. I caught a glimpse of them, as we drove in."

"Yes, Jordan, I agree," Dr. Allen nodded amiably. "I'd heard about this place from a couple of people at the clinic and planned to bring Jodie here for our anniversary, but unfortunately, that didn't happen. I hear the food is amazing."

Ian concurred, "That it is." Then he added, "This is actually the place where Peg and I finally realized we'd become more than 'friends.' I'm sure you can see how this romantic setting could do that." He smiled at his wife. "It was the perfect place to begin our life's journey together."

Peg blushed and looked away, staring intently out the window at the gardens, avoiding everyone's surprised looks.

Paul glanced around the table, not sure what he could or should say. It certainly was a romantic setting. He was thankful that he and Jordan were here with a group. Suggesting that they come here as "a couple" might have scared her away. Paul found that he still tread lightly, when it came to anything that might seem like a "date" to Jordan. Paul's musings were interrupted as the waiter returned with menus and a description of the evening's specials. The menu was varied, and everything looked delicious. Once the orders were placed, conversation resumed.

"Getting to know young Mikey as a singleton was certainly a pleasure," Paul said, choosing a safe topic. "He's very bright and inquisitive. I totally enjoyed my time with him."

"I did, too," Jordan continued Paul's thought. "He loved learning to play Chinese Checkers and was surprised to see how competitive Miss Martha was. She had him laughing and begging to play more games. Michael is such a sweet boy…and so polite. You must be so proud of him."

"He's great with BJ, too," Jodie chimed in. "Being an only child, sometimes our son has a hard time sharing, but Mikey's so patient with him. And it's a riot to hear him join Michael in the 'toys away' song. Yes, when Mikey's at our house…BJ even picks up his toys without a fuss!" She laughed good-naturedly.

"Well, thanks, you guys. We think Mikey's a pretty good kid, too," said his Dad. "Of course, both he and Mia have their moments. Sometimes when they disagree or want the same toy, they can really get after each other." Chuckling, he added, "Like all youngsters, they have to hit the 'time out chair,' once in a while."

"Seriously, though," Peg continued, "we want to thank all of you for helping us through that very challenging time. Ben and Jodie, your help and support at the Center really eased our concerns about Mia's recovery. We can't thank all of you enough…for taking care of things at school, organizing food and especially caring for Mikey. We don't know what we'd have done without you."

"That is so true…each of you is a blessing to us," Ian added, then raised his water glass. "Here's to friendship."

The couples laughed, lifted their glasses and clinked rims with their friends around the table. When conversation resumed, it shifted to focus on what each of the adults was doing. Jordan reported that her field trials were doing well and required less attention than she had expected. Ian told everyone how his father was working with a Japanese professor to track down Jatropha research currently being conducted in Japan. Paul gave the group an update on the upcoming basketball tournament and thanked them for agreeing to be part of it.

When it was the Allens' turn, they looked at each other, then looked at their friends and shared their big news – they would be welcoming a new baby in the fall! Peg literally jumped out of her seat and ran over to give her friend a big hug. "Oh, I'm so excited for you guys," she gushed, "what great news! Congratulations! What does BJ say?"

Jodie laughed, "He wants a baby brother, someone he can play trains with, like Mikey."

After chatting about baby preparations for a few minutes, Peg said that she had some good news-bad news to share about their like-family, housekeeper-babysitter, Ida. Everyone knew Ida, of course, so they were anxious to hear what was going on with her. Peg told them that Ida had accompanied a Colorado church group on a "Roads Travel Tour" of England. When she got back, she'd announced that she'd decided to move to Denver to be near her daughter. It just so happened, that on the tour she'd met a very special retired minister who'd lost his wife several years ago. And "yes," he just might be part of her future.

Everyone agreed that while that would be a huge loss for

the Mahoneys, it couldn't be better news for Ida. The group went on to talk about about the unpredictability of life and how people could never really know what the fates had in store for them.

"I guess that's why we must cherish every moment we have with our families and friends," Peg said, looking at her husband, meaningfully. He nodded, silently agreeing.

Finally, it was time to walk off those extra calories provided by the creme brulee, fresh strawberry shortcake and cherry pie a la mode. It seemed natural for the married couples to hold hands as they strolled around the Inn's lovely grounds – not surprisingly, a frequent wedding venue. Jordan couldn't help but delight in the profusion of perennials lining the walkway, resplendent in the light of the old-fashioned street lamps that lined the pathway. This was, indeed, a magical place, she thought.

"Look," said Jodie pointing up to the sliver of a moon in the darkened sky. "If we wait a minute, we just might see a falling star. Of course, you do know what that means, don't you?"

"No," said Paul and Jordan, simultaneously.

Peg and Jodie both laughed. Then Peg explained, "It's an old tradition that Jodie and I adopted when we were undergrads. If you see a falling star, you have to close your eyes and make a wish. If you're really sincere…really, really sincere…the wish will come true."

Ian joined in, "Of course, you can't tell anyone your wish…or it won't come true."

"He's got that right," emphasized Ben. "Keep looking for a falling star, Everyone…and have your wish ready."

"This is crazy," thought Jordan as she considered what she might wish for – if she believed in such myths. "Of course, if a doctor like Ben Allen and a researcher like Ian Mahoney believed it...hmmm." A wish took shape in her mind.

Then, just as she gazed up to the heavens – there was a falling star! Almost involuntarily, Jordan squeezed her eyes shut and – wished!

Paul thought it was all a big joke, but he, too, did as directed. When everyone opened their eyes, he noticed that the other fellows were hugging and kissing their wives. "What the heck," he said to himself, "why be the outlier?"

So, on impulse, he grabbed Jordan into a big bear hug and murmured, "When In Rome...." as he pecked her on the cheek. Surprise! She hadn't seemed to mind...and even smiled at his effort. "What an end to a perfect evening," he thought.

Several days later, Peg and Ian began preparing for the afternoon reception they'd be hosting in their backyard the following weekend. Ian had invited the three graduate students who were completing their degrees this spring. They'd also included their families and special friends. Ian was certainly going to miss these three – they'd not only become an integral part of his research program – they had also become his friends. It was Peg who'd suggested the reception, and Ian had readily agreed.

David Mason, the new Dr. Mason, was proud to introduce his fiancée, Alice Barber, who came all the way from Texas to witness his hooding. David would soon be joining Alice at Texas A & M for a "post doc" assignment. Unfortunately, his parents hadn't been able to make the trip, but Alice had taken a lot of photos, so folks at home could share the excitement of David's big day.

Christian Rosario's parents were in Africa, so they wouldn't see him receive his Master's Degree, either. However, his substitute family, Pastor Becky, Rod, Libby and Bob, were all there to honor his achievement. Surprising everyone, he'd recently decided to enroll in a Michigan Seminary this fall with the goal of becoming an agricultural missionary back in his birth country of Mozambique. Ian knew it was hard for Christian to leave his research and the lab work he so-loved. But Chris had shared his decision-making dilemma with Ian earlier that month. Ian now understood Christian's seemingly detached and "strange" behavior during and after his trip to Africa. He'd been struggling with his decision. But, he had confided in Ian, after much soul-searching, meditation and prayer – his true calling had become clear. He was now confident that he had made the right decision.

The third graduate to be celebrated that day was Dana Walters. "No, I'm not going to continue in a doctoral program," she announced to the group. "I've accepted a position in Washington as the Senior Administrative Assistant to the Chair of the House Agricultural Committee. I'm very excited to be going where policy is made…I'm hoping to be able to do my part to make a difference. Perhaps, sometime down the road, I may even apply to law school."

Meeting Dana's parents, an Iowa farm couple, reminded Peg of the pride her farmer parents had shown when she and her brothers achieved their academic goals. She knew that she and Ian would one day experience that same joy when they watched Mike and Mia walk across the stage to receive their diplomas and, hopefully, go on to fulfilling careers.

For Ian, the day was a time of mixed emotions. He would certainly miss the diverse expertise of these fine, talented grad students. He was grateful to them for their expertise and tireless energy on behalf of the Jatropha project. He was also proud that he had played – even a small role – in their academic success and promising futures. Today's gathering was bringing closure to what was a productive and meaningful two-year commitment among them all. He was looking forward to continuing to support each of them on his/her life's journey.

Now, Ian must, once again, build a team that would move him closer to the conclusion of his research project. But this time, rather than starting from scratch, he would be able to begin with an eager, talented, seasoned, already-committed team member – in the person of Jordan Taylor. Ian knew he could count on Jordan to challenge his ideas and be a willing lab partner, someone whose diligence equaled his own. He was confident that with her help – and the addition of a few talented grad students – the long-awaited breakthrough might just be closer than they thought.

CHAPTER TWENTY-SIX

The week after University graduation and the end of the Montessori term, Paul and Jordan had some time to work out the final details of the kids' basketball tournament. They were together almost constantly the entire week. They often met from early morning until way past dinnertime on many days.

They were busy figuring out details for the facility, custodial coverage, seating and a myriad of other considerations. Paul was also finalizing the new rules for alternating boy-girl quarters and skill-level substitutions. He wanted to be sure they hadn't missed any glaring weaknesses. They had put on a training workshop for the coaches who had, in turn, been teaching the kids. The teams had been practicing for a couple of weeks. It was too late for any major changes at this point. Jordan's assignment was to clarify the guidelines to be used by the referees.

Fortunately, Peg had taken care of ordering t-shirts for the eight different teams. She'd decided on bright colors and ordered sizes designated by each team's coach. The school secretary had been a great help, coordinating the effort. Now the shirts were in boxes, stacked in the school office. Coaches would be picking them up when they came for scrimmage game day.

"How are we coming with recruiting refs?" Jordan asked.

"Do we have enough volunteers? I know Peg was contacting the public and parochial schools to solicit names. Has she had any luck with them?"

"As a matter of fact, she and I've come up with a list of eight men and six women who're committed, plus a couple of extras who said they'd help, if needed. Directresses from the local Montessori schools are willing to ref, as are several men and women from the Singles Can group. The remainder of the volunteers came from the parochial schools and a couple of high schoolers. We decided not to ask the home-school group, since they really don't have volunteers who aren't parents. Several of those parents will be serving as timers and score keepers, though," Paul reported. "Most of the volunteers were excited about the proposed rules, and they're anxious to be a part of the program."

Paul then asked her about ref training for the volunteers. "How are you going to organize the training sessions, Jordie? I think we agreed that they'd take place here on a couple of successive Saturdays, right?"

"Well, these are volunteers, and, again, it's not the NBA… so I want to make it as convenient for them, as possible. I thought that we'd schedule two Saturdays of training sessions here at the school. Volunteers could choose the one that works best for them. If we had a 9-12 and 1-4 the first Saturday and a 9-12 the second Saturday, that would give people plenty of options. They will have the rules in advance, so we will begin by going over them and answering any questions they may have."

She had developed a simple hand-out outlining the rules which she handed to Paul for his perusal. She also threw out the idea of videotaping some of the kids during a practice. That way, the trainees could practice their officiating skills by watching the kids play and coming to a general agreement about what they should and should not call. During the final hour of training, Jordan proposed that some of the teams could come to the school for a practice, and the officials-in-training would fine-tune their skills with real kids on the court.

Once, again, Paul was impressed. The training plan made perfect sense, and he was confident the officials would be ready – not only for the tournament – but for league-play, as well.

By the end of the week, everything was ready for scrimmage game day – two games would be played in the morning and two in the afternoon. Each shortened game would take about 45 minutes. Paul had spent time with the coaches and each of the teams to ensure common understanding of the rules. The teams had been practicing over the course of the past month – dribbling, passing and shooting. Some had played informal games among themselves. And several of the teams had accepted the invitation to play during referee training. This Saturday's scrimmage game day was a way for the players to get a feel for the game when two teams were actually competing…with referees, scorekeepers and timekeepers. Paul and Jordan were serving as the refs for the day's drills. Peg and Ian would be there to hand out t-shirts and oversee the team-name drawing. They would also keep time and the score.

"I think we've taken care of everything on my list," said an exhausted Paul Friday evening as they munched Tacos on Jordan's patio.

Jordan was confident that the scrimmage game day would be fun for everyone and good practice for the upcoming tournament.

She was right. The scrimmages were a lot of fun. Parents and coaches pitched in to help hand out shirts, direct kids, supervise those waiting to play…and just do whatever needed to be done. The teams were excited about the names they had chosen and couldn't wait to start creating mascots.

After a flurry of early fouls and out-of-bound balls in game one, the kids (and officials, Jordan and Paul,) settled into an easy, relaxed rhythm. The games were not overly competitive, and after some maneuvering – the skill-based, substitution plan worked quite well. No group of kids on the court was overly-matched by their opponents. It took some coordination and agreement among opposing coaches, but they all concurred it made for safer, fairer games. All in all, the day was a huge success, and the teams were ready for the tournament which would take place in a couple of weeks.

And what a hectic couple of weeks it was. Both Paul and Jordan spent mornings at their respective workplaces, but, because their schedules were reduced during the summer, they both had much more free time later in the day. The two had found reasons – maybe actually excuses – to spend afternoons and evenings together, supposedly talking about the basketball league and upcoming tournament. But they did so, while enjoying a number of summer activities, both on campus and in the community. "That's what friends do," they told themselves, quick to agree that it was not really "dating," of course.

One evening, they joined the Allens, Mahoneys and the three children for a tour of the MSU Children's Garden and ice cream at the MSU Dairy Store. Another night, they took sandwiches, folding chairs and Martha Webb to enjoy the carillon concert on campus. Still another time, they ended up touring the State Capitol, after they both admitted they'd never been there.

Early the next week, Paul had volunteered to help weed Jordan's and Martha's garden. The latter treated them to a chicken salad supper on her patio. They went to a movie and an outdoor theatre event. They donned their helmets and explored the maze of bike paths that crisscrossed the area. They even took Mike and Mia to the community pool and splash pad one afternoon.

Late in the week, as Jordan and her neighbor relaxed on the patio with frosty glasses of iced tea, Martha observed, casually, "You and Mr. Franklin seem to be working together quite a bit. That basketball program must be quite complicated."

Jordan blushed, "Well, yes, we have been working on the basketball league and tournament, but, we've been doing other things, too. You know that, of course…are you just teasing me?"

Martha laughed, "Well, I'd have to be blind and deaf not to notice how well the two of you get along. When we were weeding the gardens, Paul was certainly attentive to your words…and your cute cutoffs. I really like Paul, and I know my husband, George, would have liked him, too. In a way… he's kind of old-fashioned."

"That's actually true, Martha," Jordan agreed. "I feel amazingly comfortable around him. There's a nice…I don't know…camaraderie, I guess…between us. Maybe it's because he, like my brother, gets a kick out of teasing me. Then too, we really like to play pickup basketball together. We're pretty well matched, but I know he holds back, just to make it competitive. He is four inches taller than I am and has played semi-pro, after all. But I know he respects my game, and not only do we get a good workout…we have fun."

"My, my," Martha said, slyly, "could this be the same gal who moved in next door last fall? What a difference a year makes! You were so man-averse, when you first moved in. You wanted nothing to do with dating, or men, in general.

And I remember the first time you met Paul…you literally ran away from him, if I recall correctly."

Jordan looked at her neighbor, a little embarrassed. "You're right, of course. I guess I have to admit, I was what they used to call, an 'ice maiden.' If I can be totally honest, Martha, dear, I think I was literally afraid to have a man for a friend. I think I was petrified of the idea of dating."

"Why-ever was that?" asked her surrogate grandmother.

"Okay…true confession time, My Friend." Jordan took a deep breath, then went on, "The truth is, my love life had been 'zilch,' Martha. When I was in high school, we mostly hung around in groups, not much pairing off…at least not in my crowd. I remember that one time, when I told my mom that a boy commented on a blouse I was wearing, I was shocked by her reaction. She was furious. Looking back, I'd say her response was…almost psychotic!"

"What did she say, Jordan, if you don't mind my asking?" her friend probed gently.

Jordan paused. She still felt guilty when saying anything that might be construed as critical of her mother. Then, she squared her shoulders and responded. "I remember her words as clearly as if she said them yesterday. She said, 'Watch out for him, Jordan. He's got something on his mind, you need to avoid. He was probably looking down your blouse and wanted to get his hands on you! That's what all men want…just to get you into bed! Stay clear of him! I know what I'm talking about!'"

"Oh, My Dear…" began Martha.

Jordan interrupted, almost defensively, "I remember that blouse very clearly…who could forget any part of that traumatic day. The blouse had a sweetheart neckline and wasn't very low, at all. The boy was just being nice. I'm sure, now, that he hadn't meant anything salacious. But at the time, I was very shy and totally intimidated by my mother. I never knew why she had such an almost violent reaction, but I thought she must know what she was talking about. She scared me away from boys for the rest of my high school years."

"So, Jordan, did you ever have a serious beau…maybe in college?" Martha asked.

"No, not really," Jordan admitted. "I never went with anyone at Purdue, if that's what you mean. There was one guy I spent some time with, though. For a while, I wondered if we might actually start to date our senior year in Lafayette."

"So, what happened, did he finally ask you out?"

Jordan answered, "Well, no. You see, most of our one-on-one time was after our religion class my Junior year. We actually had some great conversations over Cokes in the union. I confided in him my doubts about religion. I remember telling him that I just could not believe in a God who would allow bad things to happen to good people… like my father's tragic death, and the accident that ended my playing career. He listened, he counseled, he told me I had to have faith. Faith! Can you believe that? Anyway, perhaps it was my need for salvation that reinforced his decision not to return for our senior year."

"What? Whatever do you mean, My Dear?" asked her perplexed neighbor.

"You'll never believe it!" Jordan told her. "I got a letter from James over that summer. He told me he'd decided to transfer to Notre Dame! He said he had a 'calling' and decided to go to seminary to become a Catholic priest. Our discussions about religion obviously helped him more than they had me."

"Ah, that answers a lot of questions," Martha said, taking Jordan's hand. "So, that not only reinforced your objections to men…but to church, as well." Martha shook her head. "I know you were very close with your dad, but did you ever tell him about what your mother had said?"

"That's one of my greatest regrets, Martha," Jordan said. "I was too embarrassed to tell him, when it happened. Then, as I got older, I didn't want to hurt my parents' relationship, by telling him that story. The whole thing is so confusing to me. My dad was such a great guy, beloved by all. Is there a chance, he never saw that side of my mother?"

"Well, who knows," Martha said gently. "Sometimes love really is blind. Perhaps he never did see that side of her. She may have hidden it from him. Perhaps she was jealous of him, because everyone thought he was so wonderful. Or maybe she was jealous of you, because of your relationship with your father. After he died, I remember you said your mother totally withdrew from both you and your brother. I think your mom must have had some deep emotional or psychological problems. I hope she gets help to resolve them someday." She gently patted Jordan's hand. "One thing is certain, though, she sure raised a pretty remarkable daughter…in spite of her failings."

Jordan's eyes instantly filled and overflowed down her cheeks. "Oh, Martha, you are so very dear. You now know my whole sorry tale…as no one else does. And you accept me…anyway."

"Accept you?" admonished her friend, "I love you, My Dear. You are my granddaughter…and I love you just the way you are…don't ever forget that."

Jordan reached her arms around the old lady and wrapped her in the tightest hug she could muster.

"Once, again, you have saved me, Dear Martha," Jordan continued, after wiping away her tears and forcing a lop-sided smile. "They say that confession is good for the soul, so mine should be in A+ condition right now. Perhaps, admitting all this…sharing this burden I've been carrying for so long, will help me. You never know, it may just start me on a more normal trajectory."

"There's something I want you to consider, Jordan, dear," Martha said cautiously. "I know you don't believe in God… but think about this: You were blessed with the most wonderful, amazing father for twenty years of your life. You also have a brother who loves you dearly. Somehow, you gathered the strength to succeed professionally. And I was brought into your life. Do you really think all of those things are coincidences? All I ask you to do…is think about it. Could there possibly be a higher reason for all of those good things in your life? One final question: What would your father want you to believe?"

Jordan didn't say anything. She was momentarily speechless. She got to her feet, hugged her friend, again, and headed for the door. Turning, she murmured, "Thank you, Martha, I will think about everything you said. Thank you for everything!"

After her friend closed the door, Mrs. Webb took a deep breath and let it out slowly. Had she gone too far? Jordan did say she'd think about her words. She looked up at the sky and said reverently, "Thank you, Lord!"

Martha now understood the fractured life of the young woman she had come to love. How sad that her mother had so many issues…and how inexcusable it was that she had instilled fear and uncertainty in her daughter about men. It was sad, too, that Jordan's mother hadn't enveloped her daughter in love and reassurance after her father's death. It was a missed opportunity to make things right and to help each other.

Martha was surprised that Jordan had taken her mother's hateful words so much to heart. Jordan had been close to her brother, so she must have known his friends…they weren't stalking girls. And her mother certainly didn't think her own son, Bill, was "one of those predatory" males. Martha began to wonder if, perhaps, Jordan's mother – or someone close to her – had had a bad experience related to sex as a teenager. Her reaction to the blouse comment seemed so over the top, but also, apparently, isolated.

She decided she would continue to pray that in time the answers would surface. She would pray that the rift between mother and daughter would heal and that the family would, once again, become whole.

CHAPTER TWENTY-SEVEN

Tournament weekend finally arrived! All the careful planning had really paid off. The prep sessions with the youngsters had been time consuming, but Paul was glad the young competitors had made progress in learning the basic skills and were eager to compete in the two-day event. Jordan was also pleased at the response of her volunteer referees. She told Paul that she was amazed at how generous the Singles Can men and women had been with their time – and they were a lot of fun. She may have misjudged the kind of people they were. Perhaps she should consider joining this group, even though they were church-affiliated.

Arranging the tournament schedule had been a challenge, especially since the last rounds were scheduled for a Sunday. It was not the organizers' preference, but it was what the participating coaches voted to do. All eight teams would play on Saturday. Each quarter would last for seven minutes. Losing team members would each receive a red ribbon; winning team members would get blue ribbons.

The first game on Saturday would begin at 10:30 with the others following at 11:30, 1:30 and 2:30.

The semi-final games would be at 12:30 and 1:30 on Sunday with the final game starting at 3:00. Players who lost their semi-final games would receive silver medals, and the runners-up would get gold medals. Members of the championship team would each receive a small trophy. For most of these kids, this would be their first such award.

Friday afternoon Paul picked his dad up from the airport. He had flown in from Florida for a week's visit. At the apartment, they met up with Amy and her husband, Jeff, who had driven in from Virginia. "Hey, Baby Bro," teased his sister, "how'd you ever manage to set up a tournament and a basketball league your very first year in Michigan without my help? I thought you couldn't do anything without me!"

Their dad shook his head, "Some things just never change," he said indulgently. "Paul, I'm so sorry your mother couldn't be here for this. She loved her hoops, and she'd have been so proud to see all you've done to become part of your new community...and all you've done for kids!"

"I can't wait to see your school and meet your colleagues, Paul," Amy said checking out his apartment and making herself right at home.

Just then the doorbell rang. Paul opened the door and took a large container from Peg, who was standing on the porch. He then ushered her into the living room. One arm still cradling a second container, Peg gave the small group a jaunty wave and said, cheerily, "Hi, there, Franklin Family! Welcome to Michigan! I'm Peg Mahoney, one of Paul's Montessori colleagues." Handing Paul the other container, she said, "Paul, I just dropped by to bring you some gzpacho and scones that Ida made this morning. She thought you'd be way too busy to cook today, and she wanted you to have something special for the family." Turning back to the others, she continued, "It was great to meet you, Mr. Franklin, Amy, Jeff…we look forward to seeing you tomorrow and hearing some juicy stories about Paul, here." She winked and waved again, as she hurried back out the door.

Paul smiled proudly. "She and her husband, Ian, are

probably my closest friends. They were the first to welcome me when I got here last fall, and we do a lot together. They also have a set of twins who are in the school. Really, though, you won't believe what a great community this is. People are always eager to get involved in things and help each other. Wait until you see how many people have volunteered to help tomorrow. I'm so glad you three are here to be a part of all this."

"Well, I can tell I like Peg already," noted his sister. "And we wouldn't have missed your big basketball debut tomorrow for anything!"

Paul then told them about the special help he'd received from the Singles Can group at church, especially a woman named Tammy Sue. Amy recalled Paul mentioning her at Christmas. Wasn't he dating her at that time? But her brother went on talking about others who had stepped up to help, as well. He kept mentioning "Jordan," the same woman whose name had come up often over the past couple of months in their phone calls. Paul explained that it was she, who had trained the referees, helped come up with the game rules and really served as "Girl Friday" throughout the planning and execution of the whole project.

"So, is Jordan part of the Singles Can group at the church?" Amy wanted to know.

"Nah," Paul stated simply, "church is not really her thing!"

Across town, other visitors were also arriving. Jordan's brother, Bill and his wife, Maggie, had driven in from Indiana. What fun Bill and Paul's dad, another coach, would have sharing stories and probably complaining about the referees she'd trained. She looked forward to meeting Paul's sister too. She knew Paul thought the world of Amy. They seemed like such a great family.

Remembering Martha's words, Jordan said to herself,

"Be thankful for what you've got, Jordan! You and Bill have NEVER been closer!"

The Senior Mahoneys had also arrived from South Carolina, and their big news was that they planned to look at housing options in the Okemos-East Lansing area. Being so far away from their family had ceased to be an acceptable option. The kids were just growing up too quickly, and they didn't want to miss any of it!

The Gerbers, their oldest son, J. R., and his soon-to-be bride, Lindsay, would arrive in time for tomorrow's games. And, of course, all their local friends (the Lanes, Ida, Martha and the Allens) were on board for the entire weekend, as well.

Mike and Mia were both excited to be part of this big, summer event. Mia wouldn't be playing, of course, since her leg had been in a cast throughout the practice months, but she had insisted on being Ojibwa's unofficial cheerleader.

"I wish you were playing, too, Mia," complained her brother. "I know you'd be the best dribbler of all the girls… and the boys, too, probably! Our team could use your shooting." Even in her cast, Mia had continued to launch balls into the hoop on the driveway, even though she had to stand in one place while leaning on a crutch. Her brother had run around shagging the balls for her…so she'd really perfected her shot. "Next year you'll be the star!" Mike said, proudly. "I just know it!"

Mike's obvious adoration of his sister, warmed her heart – and made her feel a little guilty.

"Mikey, why are you so nice to me, when I've been kind of mean since my accident? I know I complained a lot, because I couldn't play," she confessed. "I'm sorry, Mikey. You've been so good to me…I wouldn't trade you for anybody else in the whole world!"

Mike looked at his sister strangely. She'd never talked to him like that before. He didn't really know what to say. Then the words just blurted out, "I was scared, Mia. When you fell off Lady, then just laid there with your leg looking so weird, I was afraid you might not get better. At night I cried and cried and asked God and our Guardian Angel Mommy to please make you well and strong again. I promised that if you got better, I'd be nice to you. It was a deal I made with God and Mommy."

Ian and Peg had come to just outside the door, and they had overheard Michael's words. They looked at one another, grabbed each other's hand and felt the tears come, unabashedly.

Mia patted her brother gently and said, "Wow, Mikey, really? That's amazing…so it was really YOU who made me better? I know the doctors helped, but I should have been thanking not only God…but you and Mommy, too! Thank you, Mikey, you're the BEST! Tomorrow, I'm going to cheer my loudest for you! You'll be my winner, no matter what happens with the games!"

Peg and Ian smiled at each other, then quietly slipped away.

The sun shone brightly on that gorgeous morning in July, as the teams assembled for their busy day of basketball. The Purple Carrot food truck was parked outside and ready to feed the hungry players and their fans. The host school had cases of bottled water in a small tent that provided a bit of shade. Kids were climbing and swinging on the playground equipment, while parents watched from benches and bag chairs. As the time for tipoff approached, families began to move inside. The ribbons and championship trophies were on display in the lobby where everyone could see them as they made their way to the gymnasium.

Miss Grace, Ojibwa's longtime school administrator, welcomed the guests and expressed appreciation for the community support that had enabled the youngsters from so many different educational programs to share in this special event. Finally, she named the participating schools, identified other groups who were serving as officials and thanked the sponsors who had covered the cost of t-shirts, water and awards. Everyone stood as the National Anthem was played on the PA system, and then it was time for the games to begin!

The Lynx defeated the Bobcats in Game One. The Panthers stole a close one from the Pumas in Game Two. In Game Three, it took overtime for the Cheetahs to take the Jaguars, and the Leopards were victorious over the Ocelots in the final game of the afternoon.

The medical team volunteers rotated in and out of the gym. Ben, Jodie, Dr. Wang and several nurses took turns ensuring emergency assistance was available, should the need arise. An ambulance service was on call, as well, in a case of an accident or other medical problem. The day was quite hot and the gym not air-conditioned. The school had set up big fans and opened all outside doors to get air movement in the gym. Fortunately, there was a nice breeze outside.

As coaches called the names of each team member, Trustees from Ojibwa's Board passed out the ribbons after each game. Every child was recognized for his/her effort, which was an important part of the program. Therefore, in this tournament – all children were winners!

Paul, Jordan and their families were the last to leave the school that afternoon. The volunteer cleanup crews had done a good job of policing the area – inside and out – emptying trash bins, recycling soft drink and water bottles and making sure everything was ready for the finals the next day. Paul took everyone on a quick tour of his room and the school before locking up for the night.

Meanwhile, Martha was preparing to host a picnic in her backyard for the two families. Jordan had suggested including Paul's family, since she thought the two coaches, Paul's dad and her brother, would enjoy talking hoops…and Jeff, Amy's husband, was a basketball enthusiast, as well. She also wanted to get to know Paul's sister better; they'd had very little time to talk during the tournament – Jordan had just been too busy. She was happy to notice that her sister-in-law, Maggie, had really hit it off with Amy. They were about the same age, she thought, and they were chatting away amiably on the patio, as the guys gathered by the grill. As she gazed around at the group, Jordan had a warm feeling inside. She went into the kitchen to help Martha bring food out to the picnic table. Martha had prepared potato salad, veggies and a big bowl of fruit. Paul was in charge of grilling hot dogs and hamburgers. Martha's famous brownies would round out the perfect summer meal. Finally, they all settled around the big table to enjoy the picnic…and each other.

Meanwhile, the Mahoneys, Gerbers, Lanes and Allens shared a similar gathering on Ottawa Drive. No homemade food for this group, though. There was certainly no time for that. Instead, everyone eagerly dug into the Kentucky Fried Chicken and fixings, they'd picked up on the way home from the school. After eating their fill, the twins and BJ ran to the driveway to shoot hoops. They even fashioned a basket that BJ could reach, by taking an old flower basket they found in the garage and placing it on top of their wagon.

The adults chattered on about the tournament and how well it had gone so far. Conversation soon turned to reminiscences about their last backyard gathering here – just one year ago, when the newlyweds had returned from their honeymoon. So much had happened since then: Mia's accident, J.R. and Lindsay's engagement, Jodie's pregnancy, Ian's research successes, the senior Mahoney's decision to move back to Michigan – and, of course, all the new friends they'd made. Peg and Ian's thoughts shifted to Paul and Jordan. They couldn't help but wonder what was happening at the other picnic over in East Lansing.

After dinner, the Gerbers left with the Allens, who had invited them to stay at their house that night. The Lanes headed next door. Finally, all the Mahoneys hit the hay, and the house was quiet, at last. Not being able to sleep, Ian wandered into the kitchen for a midnight snack where he encountered his father, standing by the sink with a glass of water.

"Hey, Son, I thought you'd be long asleep by now," his father said.

"Yeah, me, too," Ian replied. "Guess I'm just too keyed up after the games and the picnic."

"Want to sit and talk for a few minutes? I actually have some news for you," Big Mike said, sparking Ian's interest.

"Yeah, I know, you said you were moving back to Michigan," Ian responded.

"No, it's not that. I wanted to talk to you about our neighbors, Bert and Yoshimi."

"Oh?" asked Ian, his curiosity fully aroused.

"Remember I told you I'd spoken with them about their contacts at the university in Japan and asked them if they knew of anyone who was working on the Jatropha project?" his dad began. "Well, just this week, they stopped over with news. Apparently, one of the bio-chemistry scientists there, a Dr. Haru Yamanaka, had formerly worked on a project with the lead investigator of their Jatropha genetic research. It turns out that Yoshimi not only knows Dr. Yamanaka, but she's worked with him. So, she contacted him to get the name of the Jatropha researcher."

"Wow, Dad, that's great news," Ian said, sitting up taller and moving to the edge of the couch.

"But, that's not all," Big Mike went on. "You're not going to believe this, but it seems that Dr. Yamanaka was supposed to join the bio-chemistry faculty at MSU in January! Because of a family emergency, however, he'd had to postponed his move until August. He should be arriving here within the month!"

Ian could not believe his ears. This was almost too coincidental to be true! Direct ties to Japanese Jatropha research – right here at MSU? Now Ian understood why Jordan hadn't been able to connect with the new bio-chem professor. She'd contacted the department in February, only to be told that the professor hadn't arrived, as planned, but had been delayed for a semester. She was planning to make further contact, once the fall semester began. Now, perhaps, Yoshimi could negotiate an introduction; and he and Jordan could make the contact together.

He could not thank his father enough. This just might prove to be the key to solving his genetic puzzle. Hugging his father warmly, Ian finally said goodnight and headed up to bed. His mind reeling, Ian could not go to sleep. Then, he took a moment to calm himself, take a few deep breaths and think more clearly. Why should he be surprised, he asked himself. God had touched his life in mysterious ways many times before. This might just turn out to be one more of those times. With that, he fell deeply asleep.

Sunday turned out to be another beautiful day – a little cooler, but still the sun shone brightly. Since it was summer, Pastor Becky presided over a single, 8:30 service at the Chapel. As always, the pews were filled, and extra folding chairs had been set up in the back. Martha Webb had been coming to the Okemos Chapel, ever since she started working with Rod Lane on his book. So, before everyone had left the picnic, yesterday, she'd invited her guests to join her there for the service. She blinked at the response from Bill and Maggie Taylor. "Of course, we'll join you," Bill said, appreciatively, as Maggie nodded beside him. He turned to Jordan, "Won't we, sis?"

Jordan hadn't even batted an eye when she'd quickly responded, "Sure we will, Martha. We'll see you at 8:30 sharp!"

"Don't worry, Martha, we'll be there too," the Senior Mr. Franklin had chimed in. "Can't miss hearing that choir my son's talked about so much…and I'm also anxious to hear Pastor Becky. I really enjoyed meeting her at the tournament."

After church, everyone headed home to change, then gathered, again, at the school. Thank goodness it was a little cooler, today, everyone agreed. And before they knew it, it was time for the games to begin. How those children did play! The officials had to call only a few fouls. Of course, there were occasional traveling violations and frequent turnovers when passes inevitably missed their targets. But, thankfully, there were, again, no injuries. The medical volunteers had had an easy time of it.

On the whole, the games were well-played for such young kids. The scores were close which delighted the spectators. The Lynx played the Panthers, and the Cheetahs challenged the Leopards in the semi-finals. After a short breather, it was time for the final game of the tournament. It, too, turned out to be a very close game. In the final game, though, it was the Panthers who reigned victorious over the Cheetahs – by two, buzzer-beating points. The crowd cheered, and there were high-fives all around. You'd have thought it was the NBA finals! Paul invited Jordan to assist in the distribution of the awards for the championship teams.

One can only wonder about the discussions that took place that evening among the various family groups. There was so much to think about – weddings, babies, new friends, new experiences, promises to get together again, soon. And what about Paul and Jordan? Those who knew and loved them, sensed that things had changed between them. Amy thought Jordan was the kind of challenge that would bring out the best in her kid brother. Martha thought Paul just might be the person who could help Jordan heal her deep, personal wounds and allow her to show the world the dear, caring person Martha'd come to know and love. Ian and Peg hoped their two friends could find happiness – perhaps, together? For everyone who knew Paul and Jordan, however, the question remained: would the couple ever be able to… Give Love a Chance?

CHAPTER TWENTY-EIGHT

The rest of July and the month of August came and went. Jordan took Paul to visit her field trials, a new experience for the city lad who wasn't into gardening and even less into ornamental grasses and scientific trials. But Jordan was a patient and helpful instructor, and Paul turned out to be an eager student. She had spent so much time with him in his world, it was a real pleasure for him to experience hers. Paul was quick to see how Jordan's scientific mind worked and recognize how bright and capable she was. It was no wonder she was on such a successful career track.

One Saturday, they went to Grand Rapids and toured the Meijer's Gardens. They also went with the Singles Can group for a week-end trip to Mackinaw Island. Since it was an overnight, Tammy Sue invited Jordan to be her roommate. Jordan readily accepted, and the two women had a chance to get to know each other. They shared their interests and joys and challenges of their careers.

Tammy Sue confided in Jordan that she and her old friend from Atlanta had rekindled their relationship and were even thinking of a long-term commitment. "We are so alike," Tammy said. "Sometimes I think timing is everything. When Mark and I knew each other in Atlanta, we were both so career-focused, we had little time left for each other. But, here things are different. We just seem to have 'clicked.' Do you know what I mean?" Tammy Sue asked.

"Yes, Tammy Sue," Jordan answered slowly, "I think I do."

A few days after they returned to Okemos, Paul invited Jordan to meet one afternoon in the school's greenhouse to talk with the students about what they were growing and what products they might be able to make and sell at their road-side market. The children warmed to Jordan and asked her dozens of questions. She smiled and answered each of them patiently and kindly. Paul watched her interact with the children. He had to admit, she was a natural. As a thank you, Paul took her to a small Italian restaurant that he enjoyed. Their conversations always varied. Sometimes they laughed and told funny stories; other times they talked about deep personal issues, and other times they debated social and political issues. A few things were becoming clear to them both: they were completely comfortable with one another, they respected each other and each cared deeply for the other.

Paul continued to visit possible sites where he might build his dream house. On many occasions, Jordan accompanied him. They had endless discussions about just what kind of house he should build.

"I don't want to build anything like the stuffy old historic houses in Virginia where I grew up," he said adamantly. "No white columns and ornate chandeliers for me. I much prefer the clean lines of a more "Frank Lloyd Wright Prairie-Style" home with lots of built-ins and open spaces. There are actually a lot of them in this area. Maybe we could go on a home tour sometime to see them," he suggested.

"Paul," Jordan replied, "I've toured a number of Wright-style houses. There was one near the Purdue campus. And one weekend Val and I did a home tour outside Chicago, where we saw several. I do like their clean lines and how they sort of build the home into the landscape."

"But I bet you like something more traditional, don't you?" he wanted to know.

"Well, maybe. I've always liked log houses or A-frames. Our home in Indiana was in a sub-division where there were only two kinds of homes: two-story, four-bedroom colonials and three-bedroom, one car ranches...so boring! They all looked alike. What made some of them a bit unique, was their attractive landscaping and gardens," she admitted.

They both acknowledged that they liked neighborhoods where there was variety in home styles. They also agreed it might be nice to live in the country...perhaps with an acre or two.

"Wouldn't it be great to have space for both a flower and a vegetable garden in the yard?" Jordan mused aloud.

As summer turned into fall, the two found themselves spending more and more time together. They were slowly thinking of each other as much more than friends.

Paul was not known for his patience, but where Jordan was concerned, he was willing to bide his time. He knew in his heart that she was becoming more and more a part of his life...and...he was beginning to hope...his future. One night, while watching the flames of a campfire Paul had built on his patio in a portable firepit, Jordan told him the painful story about her high school experience with her mother. She told him about the tragedies of her Purdue years. She openly admitted that those experiences had somehow scared her away from both relationships and religion.

But Jordan had also tearfully admitted, "Paul, I want to trust. I desperately want to believe. Do you think there's any hope for me?"

That night, Paul had taken her in his arms and held her

tight. "You, Dear Jordan, have so much life…so much love inside of you. Do not worry…trust, faith, even love will come to you. In fact, I believe they're already inside you."

Paul was wise enough to understand that he didn't know everything that was behind her resistance to trust, faith and love. But he had seen her soften over time. It had been a slow metamorphosis…but it was happening.

"I believe she trusts me," Paul told himself. "She enjoys our time together. We both love kids, and she has willingly joined Singles Can. She even comes to church on a semi-regular basis."

Jordan had noticed the change in herself, as well. The night she'd told Paul her deepest secrets…a huge, impenetrable wall seemed to vanish. As he'd held her, she'd felt safe, free of fear and even…just maybe…loved.

Jordan recalled that Peg had once told her in confidence that her one regret was that she and Ian had not really dated very much. They somehow built a strong wonderful friendship doing things they both felt strongly about – things like youth group activities, lots of child-centered activities, time with their families. It was actually, when Peg had stepped in to care for Ian's children while he was in Africa that their relationship had changed. In fact, Peg had told her, it was the twins who were the real matchmakers. Jordan chuckled as she recalled hearing that the twins had actually initiated Ian's proposal. A proposal that had invited Miss Peggy to marry all three of them! The wedding and honeymoon had all happened before they had known each other for even one full year.

Labor Day came and went. Fall classes began for both of them, but they continued to find reasons to be together. As the anniversary of their meeting neared, Paul finally decided it was time to approach her about a possible future together.

Ian invited Jordan to dinner at the English Inn to celebrate "one full year of friendship." Jordan readily agreed.

The dinner was perfect. The conversation easy and personal. In fact, Jordan revealed more about her mother over dinner. It seems during a recent open conversation with her brother, Bill had told her that their mother had an extremely traumatic experience, while Jordan was in high school. Jordan explained to Paul that the daughter of one of her mother's closest childhood friends had become pregnant at 16 years old. The girl had not told her mother, but, instead, had gone with her boyfriend to a nearby town to have an abortion. There were complications...hemorrhaging...and the poor girl...died. She said that she and Bill now believe the whole experience so frightened their mother, that she would do or say anything to protect her own daughter from such a fate.

Jordan simply told her story. She wasn't embarrassed or ashamed. She felt safe. She trusted Paul.

Then she said, "All these years, I've thought she hated me...and now I believe she was really trying to protect me. I suppose, in her own way, she somehow believed that I'd be better off not dating, than getting into a physical relationship that I couldn't handle. Then, when she lost Dad, I think she tried to protect me from the pain of losing the love of your life...as she had, when she lost Dad. Somehow, she must have believed that if I never loved or married, I'd never get hurt. How wrong she was. It is far more hurtful to have no love in your life...to spend your life, alone. I'm just so sad that she and I were not there for each other...that we've lost all those years of family."

Paul paused for a few moments. "I hope that one day you and your mother can find peace, forgiveness and love, once again, my dear, dear Jordan," Paul said with warmth and understanding.

"Well, you never know," Jordan said with a wry smile. "Martha recently came across an article about a huge 'find' during a dig in Central America by a new paleontologist by the name of Eve Taylor. Eve Taylor could be my mom, Evelyn Taylor! Dad even used to call her his 'Evie.' Wouldn't that be something?" she asked, then laughed. "I suppose you'd say, 'It's God working in strange and mysterious ways!'"

"Well...we'll see," Jordan said, suddenly serious. "Just maybe, you'd be right!"

With that, they finished dessert and headed for a walk in the garden. Yes, this time there was a full moon and a sky full of bright, shining stars. Just then, a star streaked across the heavens...way brighter than all the rest. Without saying a word, they clasped hands, closed their eyes and each made a wish. Then they smiled at each other knowingly, moved together and kissed...softly at first...then, more urgently. The electricity that coursed through them both was startling and all-encompassing. They kissed again, this time the depth and passion of their kiss was undeniable. All the months of hiding their feelings, avoiding contact, denying the truth...finally came crashing down upon them. They were at last free...free and admittedly...in love.

There was silence for a moment before Paul spoke, clutching both of Jordan's hands in his, he said reverently, "Jordan, I have no twins to help me out with this, but...would you... would you be willing to share your life with me? I think I've loved you since the night we met...even when you totally rejected me...it just made me want you more. I love your sass, your search for answers, your love for children, your reluctance...then your willingness to face your demons head on. I love playing basketball with you. I love laughing with you. What I'm trying to say, Sweet, Dear Jordan, is... I want you to be my wife. Will you marry me, Dr. Jordan Taylor? If you say, 'Yes,' I promise we will build a house together that fulfills both our dreams, and I know we will surely live in it…happily for ever and ever after."

"Dear, patient Paul," Jordan said, squeezing his hands, "I've known for months that my soulmate was right by my side. I wanted to say something, but we both now know why I couldn't. You put up with me…you led me by the hand…you waited for me. You have helped heal me, Paul. You've shown me what it means to be good and fair and caring in this world. You have made me whole, again. Yes, I will happily marry you, Mr. Franklin. I would be honored to be your wife. So, can we stop talking now? Kiss me, my husband-to-be!" And they moved into one another and kissed, again…then they clung together as they watched the moon and stars overhead.

Looking up, Jordan added, "I only hope your mom and my dad are watching us right now. I think they would be very happy for us both!"

"I know my mom is watching," Paul said, reaching into his pocket. "This was her engagement ring, and I know she wants no one else to wear it." With that, he slipped the beautiful diamond ring onto her finger.

As the evening ended, and their lives together began, they were both thankful that they had, indeed, finally decided to….Give Love a Chance!

AUTHOR BIOGRAPHY:

Maxine S. Ferris is an Emeritus Professor and Director of Outreach Communications at Michigan State University. A graduate of the College of Wooster, she earned a Master's Degree from The Ohio State University and a PhD from MSU. A former high school teacher, then a faculty member at the College of Wooster and Bowling Green State University, she had her own consulting firm prior to returning to university teaching. The author of six non-fiction books and more than 50 popular educational publications, "Give Love a Chance" is her second novel and the sequel to "Let Love Happen." Both are Christian romance novels. She and her husband, along with six other couples, founded the second Montessori School in Michigan in 1968 and continue to be active with its programs. It is for this reason that Montessori educators play key roles in her novels. A basketball enthusiast since her teens, basketball also plays a major role in her latest novel. Maxine and her husband, Jake, have two adult sons, a daughter-in-law and two grand-children who inspire her to keep learning and trying new things. Her home is in East Lansing, Michigan.